Provençal Inspiration

Living the French Country Spirit
Home Plans ◆ Landscapes ◆ Interiors

HOME PLANNERS, LLC
Wholly owned by Hanley-Wood, LLC
TUCSON, ARIZONA
www.eplans.com

Provençal Inspiration

Published by Home Planners, LLC
Wholly owned by Hanley-Wood, LLC
3275 W. Ina Road, Suite 110
Tucson, AZ 85741

Distribution Center:
29333 Lorie Lane
Wixom, MI 48393

Jan Prideaux, *Editor in Chief*
Kristin Schneidler, *Editor*
Laura S. Moreno, *Plans Editor*
Ashleigh E. Stone, *Plans Editor*
Paul Fitzgerald, *Senior Graphic Designer*
Teralyn Morriss, *Graphic Production Artist*

10 9 8 7 6 5 4 3 2 1

Printed in the United States of America
Library of Congress Catalog Card Number: 2001089701
ISBN softcover: 1-881955-89-3

Editor's Note

For over fifty years, Home Planners has published high-quality magazines and trade books filled with distinguished designs and innovative ideas. Now, we step into the new century with our Inspiration Series, which provides a more holistic approach to home design. Books in this series focus on creating a total home environment—the architecture, the interior furnishings and details, and even the landscaping. Each book visits a region known for its alluring atmosphere and unique design style, and offers tips on how to bring that atmosphere to your home.

The journey begins in Provence, located in southeastern France along the Mediterranean coastline. The sun-splashed beaches of the Côte d'Azur and the luxurious life of the Riviera are often the first things that come to mind when southeastern France is mentioned. Recent travel memoirs and photo essays, however, have brought the peaceful Provençal countryside, with its romantic atmosphere and distinctive style, to the forefront. Earth-toned exteriors and colorful yet harmonious interiors define the region, and the delicate details and simple furnishings adapt to any home. Full-color photography, home showcases and even information about French folk arts and regional cuisine will get you started on building your own Provençal paradise.

Get Inspired!

PROVENCE

Above: The yellow area idenifies Provence: a small corner of France that becomes more popular every day.

Right: This map shows a close-up of the six departments that make up Provence.

Maps ©Russ Collins

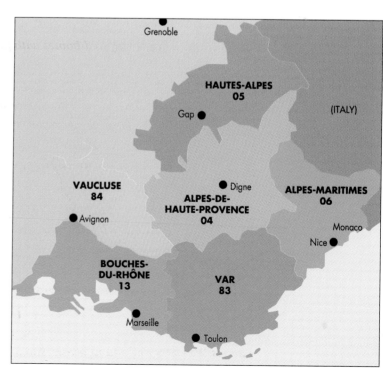

Grenoble

HAUTES-ALPES 05

Gap

(ITALY)

VAUCLUSE 84

Digne

ALPES-MARITIMES 06

ALPES-DE-HAUTE-PROVENCE 04

Avignon

Monaco

Nice

BOUCHES-DU-RHÔNE 13

VAR 83

Marseille

Toulon

Table of CONTENTS

Bienvenue!

WHAT IS PROVENCE?

Provence is not a geographical region, clearly labeled on a map—there are no French departments (administrative regions) with that name. Instead, Provence is a cultural and historical region, composed of six departments—Alpes-de-Haute-Provence, Hautes-Alpes, Alpes-Maritimes, Var, Bouches-du-Rhône and Vaucluse. From the snow-capped Alps to the balmy Mediterranean coastline, from rolling fields of lavender to vast vineyards, from the popular beaches of Saint-Tropez to quiet country cottages that are off the beaten path—Provence has a startlingly diverse appeal.

This intriguing region, inhabited for thousands of years, entered recorded history as a Greek colony (Massilia, today the city of Marseilles) over two thousand years ago; due to its coastline location, the influence of other Mediterranean cultures was strong. A few centuries later, the Romans arrived; soon after, the area was part of the Roman *provincia*, and later became known simply as Provence. Over the next thousand years, Provence was alternately ruled by the Romans, the Franks and even the Spanish. In the early 13th Century, northern France began to introduce its influence, but Provence still remained independently governed. During the French Revolution, the region lost its own political institutions, and several

Language and Literature

Due to its relative isolation from the rest of France—Provence is bordered by the Rhône river to the west, the Mediterranean to the south, and mountains to the northeast and east—Provence developed its own distinct traditions in many areas, including that of language. The regional dialect was called Occitane, or *langue d'oc*. Well suited to poetry and songs, it was the language of the medieval troubadours, who wrote of heroic deeds and courtly love; the language was also widely used by writers in other areas of Europe, particularly northern Spain. Provençal people saw their unique language as a symbol of their region's independence; however, in 1539, French was made its official language in an attempt to absorb Provence into the kingdom. The written language fell out of use, though the spoken language survived.

In 1854, author Frédéric Mistral was one of the founding members of a literary circle called the Félibrige; these writers called for a revival of the Provençal language and customs. Mistral wrote poetry, plays and novels, and spent decades compiling a dictionary of the Provençal language and traditions. In 1904, Mistral was awarded the Nobel Prize for Literature for his study of the Provençal language and his contributions to Provençal literature.

The soothing scent of lavender hangs in the air throughout Provence, playing a large role in establishing its relaxed atmosphere.

Provence has been inhabited for thousands of years; ruins such as this medieval château can be seen in many areas.

of the administrative regions we see today (Alpes-de-Haute-Provence, Bouches-du-Rhône and Var) were created. Vaucluse was added in 1791, and Alpes-Maritimes joined the rest of the departments in 1860.

The Provençal Landscape

Mountains dominate the landscape of Provence to the east and southeast. During the Middle Ages, the mountains were a place of retreat, a high, safe area where people could go to escape invasions. Often, entire towns were constructed in the peaks; today, many of these old towns have been restored and are famous for the breathtaking views that they provide. The Luberon is the main mountain range in the southeast; an extension of this range, called the Alpilles, is located between Arles and Avignon. Among the soaring peaks of the Alpilles is one of Provence's most famed mountain villages, Les-Baux-de-Provence. Accessible only by foot, Les-Baux-de-Provence is actually made up of two villages: the lower one is a still-inhabited commercial town, while the upper village is a ghost town, an uninhabited area filled with medieval ruins.

The highest peak of the region is Mont Ventoux, or "windy peak." Views from this peak are magnificent indeed; the Vaucluse Plateau to the south, the Baronnies Plateau to the north, and the Rhône Valley to the east are all visible. The foothills of the Ventoux range are remarkable as well; the western foothills are home to the vineyards that produce some of Provence's most desired wines.

The plateaus and valleys that can be viewed from Mont Ventoux have been immortalized by many painters; the Rhône Valley in particular was a subject of

The deep blue of the Mediterranean Sea gives the Côte d'Azur, or "sky-blue coast," its name.

"Provence has been accurately described as a cold country with more than its fair share of sunshine, and the climate can't seem to make up its mind whether to imitate Alaska or the Sahara."
—Peter Mayle, from "The Dangers of Provence," Salon.com

both Vincent van Gogh and Paul Cezanne. The grand city of Avignon, with its stunning examples of medieval architecture, is a part of the Rhône Valley; Arles, also located in this valley, was initially settled as a trading post and eventually became the wealthiest city in the Roman Empire, next to Rome itself. Peach and almond trees bloom prominently in Arles, and along the Vaucluse Plateau as well.

In addition to the almond trees, Vaucluse is also known for its lavender fields and ocher cliffs. In summer, the air is filled with the scent of lavender in bloom; the fragrance reaches its height during the lavender harvest in mid-August. The pale yet intense color of the blooming lavender pleases the eye, as do the majestic ocher cliffs. Through the centuries, ocher has been used to tint house paints and fabrics, and Vaucluse contains the world's largest ocher deposits. More than a dozen shades occur naturally, and the town of Rousillon displays houses colored in all variations.

The coastline of Provence includes all types of settlements, from the comfortable beaches and luxurious accommodations of the Côte d'Azur, or "sky-blue coast," to simple fishing villages. Marseilles, the largest city in Provence, is an active, bustling port; west of Marseilles is the Camargue, a marshland that serves as a wildlife preserve.

Provence: The Artists' Retreat

The beautiful landscape and tranquil atmosphere of Provence have inspired many a creative endeavor over the centuries, from the troubadour poets of the 11th Century to the travel writers and photographers of today. A number of famed 19th- and 20th-Century artists took holidays or made their homes there. Cubist painter Paul Cezanne moved from Paris to Provence in the late 19th Century, and was followed by other modern artists. Pablo Picasso spent time in the Riviera, and Henri Matisse made his home in Nice. And, in 1889, Vincent van Gogh traveled from Arles to Saint-Remy de Provence for a hospital stay, and was comforted by the serene atmosphere. Though he only spent a year in Provence, he completed more than 150 paintings there, one of them the well-known *Starry Night.*

Writers, too, have felt the allure of Provence. American author Ernest Hemingway included it in his travels, as did F. Scott Fitzgerald. British writers Somerset Maugham, Graham Greene and Katherine Mansfield also retreated to Provence, where the sun shone often and the winters were far milder than English winters. And, with the recent interest in travel memoirs, many of today's travelers find Provence a worthy place to visit, paint, photograph and reflect upon.

Wind and Weather

Much of Provence glories in a mild Mediterranean climate, but its geographical differences create plenty of weather variations. Summers are hot, during the day at least; temperatures drop somewhat at night (in the mountains, nights are always cool). The coastline is generally warmer than regions that are further inland, as well. Autumn is a warm but stormy season, and storms are fiercer in the mountains. Though the vineyards are colorful and ready for harvesting at this time, the forests, most of which are filled with evergreen trees that do not change color in fall, display gentle rather than brilliant hues. Winters are mild along the coastline, but vary inland: some areas receive snow beginning in midwinter, and areas with higher elevations, in the Alps, may get snow all winter. Once spring arrives, the weather warms up; spring can be rainy, though most downpours are quick. The mistral (Provençal for "master"), a cold, ferocious north-northwest wind, blows mostly in the spring, going through the Rhône Valley to the Mediterranean. This wind, which has reached speeds of 125 mph, can blow for days at a time; in earlier days, it was said to drive people insane.

> "The Provencal attitude toward time is that there is plenty of it. If by chance you should run out of it today, more will be available tomorrow. Or the day after. Or next week."
> —Peter Mayle, from "The Dangers of Provence," Salon.com

Day by Day

In our wireless world, we are accessible anywhere—not only in our homes and at work, but in the car, at the gym, and in restaurants and theatres. Time is of the essence, deadlines are strict, and we often skip important things, like sleeping and meals, to allow ourselves more time to work. It's no wonder that we find exotic, romantic destinations, where the pace of life is slower and there's plenty of time to relax, so appealing. The French, particularly the Provençal, are widely known for their calm attitude and appreciation of life. Long strolls and leisurely lunches, where full attention is given to the meal provided, are the order of the day here. Time is fluid, and deadlines are negotiable; life is to be enjoyed, not rushed through.

The Provençal people have faced many challenges over the centuries—perhaps the early invasions, long wars, the Crusades, and the French Revolution instilled in them the ability to live in the moment, and be grateful for what is available. Maybe it's time for us to do the same—turn our pagers off, head home a bit early, and spend the evening sharing an unhurried meal with family and friends.

The ocher deposits in Vaucluse are the largest in the world; this cliff is located in Rousillon.

THE PROVENÇAL HOME

In Provence, the typical rural residence is a low farmhouse called a *mas*, usually constructed of limestone. These mostly symmetrical homes are designed to withstand both the heat of the Provençal summer and the chill and winds of winter—in fact, most rural Provençal homes have no north-facing windows, to make sure that the powerful mistral, which comes from the north, does minimal damage. To further guard against the weather,

The village of Cotignac, located in the Var, is filled with homes that harmonize with the landscape.

This sweet French-style cottage showcases a high hipped roof, corner quoins and gently rounded dormer windows; see page 66 for more information.

the walls are thick and strong; windows are small, doors are reinforced, and chimneys are low and squat, close to the gently sloping, clay-tiled rooflines. Decorative detailing is minimal, and the homes of the countryside are often white, off-white or stone gray; however, the brilliant hues of the landscape make up for the subdued facades.

Tiled roofs also adorn the homes in larger Provençal villages or cities; these buildings are usually made of stone as well, but here the limestone is

Drystone Construction

Today, examples of an ancient method of construction dot the Provençal landscape: drystone structures, made—without mortar or other tools—of carefully placed stones. Stone is plentiful in Provence, and farmers would often need to spend time clearing stones from their fields before starting to plant. The farmers then used the stones to build low walls and small stone huts. Some larger drystone structures were actually used as dwelling places.

Drystone construction has drawn lots of attention lately—while some cement structures are already crumbling, the drystone huts (sometimes called "bories") have lasted for centuries without significant damage. Several groups have been reviewing the painstaking construction methods and admire the Provençal peasants of the past, who devoted so much time to creating these sturdy structures.

rubbed smooth and painted over in warm earth tones. Sometimes, front doors and shutters are painted with vivid colors, and window boxes are filled with colorful flowers—however, the prevailing attitude in Provence supports homes that complement the landscape and do not distract from it.

In addition to its sturdy, rural farmhouses and taller, more colorful urban homes, Provence has its share of *bastides* (spacious manor

This mas, *surrounded by a landscape rich with color, provides an example of rural homes in Provence.*

homes), castles, and other impressive buildings. Examples of Roman and medieval architecture are found in all the regions of Provence, and churches, cathedrals, abbeys and monasteries showcase a variety of architectural styles—Romanesque, Gothic, baroque, and Renaissance among them.

Adapting to America

Though Provençal home styles are well suited to their locations, adapting French styles to communities in the United States can be challenging. Regional building materials are quite different, as are weather conditions—the stone facades and tiled roofs of Provence would look out of place in most neighborhoods. Instead, individual characteristics of homes from Provence, and the rest of France as well, can be used to add French Country style.

Over the past few centuries, French styling has influenced several areas in the United States. From the early 18th Century to the late 19th Century, the French colonists shared their design preferences—particularly in the South. Many charming French Colonial homes in New Orleans, Louisiana, displayed characteristics such as stucco facades, high hipped or side-gabled roofs and tall, narrow casement windows. In rural areas, French Colonial homes often

The Mediterranean character of this plan is evident in its stone-and-stucco facade, shuttered windows and latticed front porch; see page 97 for more information.

© American Home Gallery, Ltd.

ROD DENT

COPYRIGHT LARRY E. BELK

Stone pediments, tall windows and a flower box lend French Country charm to this luxurious manor home; see page 143 for more information.

Regional Influences

America's neighborhoods display a great variety of housing styles: from the Cape Cods and Colonials of the East Coast to the rambling mansions of the South, and on to the stucco and adobe homes of the Southwest. These differences are mainly due to the regional building materials, but climate is also a factor. When the colonists arrived in America on the heavily forested East Coast, they built wood-framed homes with shingle and siding exteriors; as people traveled further west, they were introduced to materials that were appropriate for warmer, drier climates.

In France, the regional building materials and influences vary widely as well. Normandy, in northern France, has more forested area than the rest of the region, and features timber-framed homes; smaller thatched or stone houses dot the landscape in Brittany. Wooden facades with steeply sloped roofs define the homes of the Alps, where heavy rains prevail; and in Alsace, homes are colorful and decorated with gingerbread trim, much like the German homes just across the border. Provence, with its clay-tiled roofs and emphasis on earth tones, reflects a distinct Mediterranean influence.

Customs, too, influence regional architecure. In Normandy, farmers would often connect their barns and homes in order to keep a watch on their valuable livestock; feed for the animals needed to be near as well, so the grain silo was kept close. Today, many Norman-style homes feature turrets and towers, though they no longer hold grain. In the Basque area of southwestern France, homes are often three stories high. The first floor was reserved for animals, carts and other supplies; the family would live on the second floor and use the airy third floor to dry clothing and store food.

featured hipped roofs that were extended to cover wide, deep porches, which were perfect for the milder climates of the South.

In the early 20th Century, more French-inspired homes cropped up in America's neighborhoods. Usually known as "French Eclectic," this design style began when American and Canadian soldiers returned from World War I with some knowledge of French housing styles and building materials. Though French Eclectic homes often combine design elements from different parts of France, the designs share most details. French Eclectic homes feature stucco, brick or stone facades and hipped rooflines with flared eaves; most of them displayed dormer or multi-paned windows. Arched doorways and windows are common as well. Some French Eclectic homes, influenced by the cottages of Normandy, showcase decorative half-timbering, much like that of Tudor homes.

Inside

THE PROVENÇAL HOME

THE PROVENÇAL HOME
Inside

Usually, the facade of a Provençal home is simple and sub-dued—smoothed-down limestone painted over in earth tones blends with terra-cotta roof tiles. Provençal interi-ors, however, often sport quite a different look. Rich with vivid colors and tempting textures, the interior is the place to display fabrics and furnishings that mimic the brilliant hues of the Provençal landscape. The many shades of red and yellow ocher are quite popular—the ocher deposits of the Vaucluse are the largest in the world, making these two colors a natural choice—but other col-ors, such as lavender, sage green and a wide variety of blues, are also featured prominently.

Adding Provençal style to the rooms of your home requires two things: an eye for detail and an open mind. Americans are used to pur-

Preceding spread: The vibrant reds and yellows of Provence, along with a variety of country accents, brighten this living room.

Though the furnishings and fabrics of this room project a distinguished air, the nat-ural woods of the beam ceiling and hardwood floor offer a bit of relaxed country charm.

Hanging cookware, ceiling beams and a large wooden table add Provençal style to this kitchen.

These reversible quilted throws can add a splash of Provençal style to any room—use them as tablecloths, bed covers or chair throws.

Opposite: Sheer curtains, delicate pottery and a subtle blend of colors—cream, pale yellow and cool blue—create a quietly elegant look in this sitting room.

chasing sets, not pieces, of furniture—perfectly paired sofas and recliners, coordinated tables and chairs—and often use the color wheel to determine whether or not items look good together. The French, on the other hand, have little use for the color wheel, preferring to rely on instinct and imagination. Provençal style, in particular, focuses on harmony and balance, not symmetry and exact matches. Furnishings can be mix-and-match: a brand-new dining table can be accented by several antique dining chairs, and stripes, floral prints and checks can go in the same room, so long as they complement each other. Decorative details—pottery, candles, photo frames and other small accents—should help unify the larger pieces. Lighting is soft, and often natural—the French dislike track lighting, preferring to use floor lamps and carefully placed candles and sconces, and the warm Provençal sun streams freely through windows with sheer curtains. Walls, fabrics and floors are often textured, creating enticing surfaces where light can play.

The skillful blend of fabrics, furnishings and textures that composes a Provençal interior pleases the eye and the touch, while the vivid colors, inspired by nature's palette, provide a glimpse of a land where the pace of life is slower and there is always plenty of time. Add a bit of Provençal style to your home's interior, and let the harmony inspire you.

Provençal Fabrics

When envisioning a room decorated in the Provençal style, the first element that comes to mind is often the fabric. Perhaps the most distinctive aspect of Provençal design, this versatile, brightly colored and printed cotton can be used as drapery, upholstery, table linens and wall coverings. To some people, this fabric reflects the

Fabric, perhaps the most important element of Provençal style, can be found in a wide variety of colors and patterns.

Opposite: Five distinct yet complementary patterns are joined in this kitchen, where a white table setting contrasts nicely with dark woods.

Warm tones and natural light make this dinette a comfortable place for sharing meals.

very essence of Provence: the vivid colors mirror those found in the tranquil Provençal landscape, and the lightweight cotton fabric speaks of the easy, relaxed atmosphere that travelers associate with Provence.

These fabrics, called *indiennes,* originated in the East and were introduced in Marseilles by Portuguese and Dutch trading ships sometime in the early 17th Century. They were well-received, particularly by the French aristocracy—at the time, their fashionable dress consisted of heavy materials such as brocade and damask, and they were pleased to discover a lighter, more comfortable alternative. The price that they were willing to pay for importing these fabrics intrigued the craftspeople of Marseilles, who began producing them locally. These early efforts, painstakingly hand-painted, grew in popularity, and both imports and locally produced indiennes were in great demand.

In 1686, under pressure from silk and wool makers worried about losing their businesses, the government outlawed printed cotton fabrics. Naturally, this only increased their allure; a brisk smuggling business began, and the aristocracy rebelled with enthusiasm. In 1759, the ban on cotton fabrics was lifted; soon, factories began producing high-quality fabrics and even started to integrate French themes into the designs. A decade later, the people of Provence joined the aristocracy in wearing these vibrant fabrics; this became the traditional regional dress.

In the late 19th Century, production of indiennes almost ceased, though local manufacturers continued to take orders for clothing. Due to the increased popularity of some new fabrics from the north of France, demand for the indiennes had decreased. Once modern printing techniques were introduced, however, these Provençal fabrics made a comeback. By the 1950s, they were once again an integral part of many Provençal homes, and the rest of the fashionable design world took notice as well.

This dining area is made unique by floor-to-ceiling curtains, a festive table runner and mix-and-match furnishings.

Fine Fabrics

The brightly colored indiennes associated with Provence are just one of many exquisite fabrics that the French use to add flair to their homes; following are brief descriptions of some of the more exotic fabrics that are used in home decoration, and some of their advantages and disadvantages.

Brocade is a heavy fabric with a raised, often floral, design; though originally made of silk, it is now available in cotton and cotton blends.

Chenille is a soft fabric with a fuzzy texture; throws made of chenille often have fringes and tassels.

Chintz is another bright, printed fabric, made of cotton and featuring designs of flowers, fruits and birds. It is often treated with a special finish that allows it to repel dirt, and is consequently well-suited for use as curtains or upholstery.

Damask, another rich fabric, is made of alternating satin and matte, and is reversible—its versatility makes it suitable for use as upholstery, draperies and tablecloths.

Jacquard is a fabric woven on a special loom invented by Joseph Jacquard; the loom uses perforated cards to weave complicated patterns.

Linen is a fabric that is made from flax; though it is known for its strength, it tends to wrinkle easily.

Moire, a ribbed fabric, is often composed of silk or acetate.

Muslin is an extremely lightweight, gauzy fabric that can be used for curtains or bed hangings.

Silk is a smooth, fragile fabric that drapes well and can be blended with other fibers. Though it absorbs dyes well, its colors can fade when exposed to strong sunlight.

Varied shades of blue create a soothing atmosphere in this country kitchen.

Today, two Provençal companies—Souleiado and Les Olivades—are the two main producers of authentic indiennes; dozens of other companies produce fabric that incorporates Provençal patterns on everything from table linens and porcelain to clothing and jewelry.

Provençal Furnishings

For hundreds of years, Provençal homes were modest, with simple furnishings—fancy items were brought in from Paris. Then, in the early 18th Century, a newly affluent group of residents along the Rhône began building grand manors and furnishing them accordingly. Local artisans took the styles from Paris and adapted them to the countryside; the fluid lines were retained,

Often, the decor of a Provençal room revolves around one large, impressive piece of furniture, such as this weathered yet elegant china cabinet.

Opposite: Colorful stoneware, a striking border and painted chairs add country style to this sunny kitchen.

Gentle shades of rose, slate blue and sage green blend in the flowered wallpaper, which corresponds to the flower carvings on the buffet.

Plenty of tile, a colorful rug and pots of fresh herbs make this a French Country kitchen.

Opposite: Soft draperies, honey-toned woods and a rich shade of red are the highlights of this simply decorated bedroom.

but the gilt and bronze used as accents were replaced by charming country touches like shells, sculpted flowers and carved olive branches. The flowing lines and regional touches appeared on commodes (large chests-of-drawers), armoires, and some furniture items unique to the French Country life, such as a wooden, wall-mounted cage used to store bread and a table with a compartment that was used for dough preparation.

French Country furnishings are generously sized, perhaps because French Country homes were often sparsely furnished—larger sofas, tables and chairs fill up a room and make it appear more spacious as well. Styles are varied—the French had many influences when it came to furniture craftsmanship. In the early 17th Century, each region's craftspeople used a plentiful local wood to create immense pieces with clean lines and simple carvings. The baroque period followed, and with it came more elaborately carved furnishings. Design styles of the Far East also provided inspiration during the later 17th Century; the French fondness for embroidered hangings, lacquered cabinets and blue-and-white porcelain can be traced to these years.

Despite variance in furniture styles, some pieces of furniture have remained popular whether simple or elaborate. The armoire, for instance, has passed almost seamlessly

from the past into the present. Dating from the Middle Ages, when it was used to store armor, it is an essential part of the French home, and in many cases a family heirloom, passed from one generation to the next. Many French Country families kept all of their valuable possessions—clothing, tools and dinnerware—in their armoires. In northern France, armoires were usually made of oak or pine; Provençal armoires, however, were made of walnut. Armoires are easy to incorporate into today's homes; in addition to using them for clothing storage in the bedrooms, many people add armoires to their gathering rooms to conceal their television sets and stereos, so these modern appliances do not break up the look of a room furnished with antiques.

Room by Room

The main living areas of the Provençal home—the family/living room, dining room and kitchen—offer an alluring blend of sophisticated style and country charm; it's not unusual to see a family room with a rustic timbered ceiling decorated in a grand style, with elaborately carved furnishings. Living and family rooms are often a mix of formal and informal styles; dining rooms tend to be more distinguished and refined, and the kitchen is a cozy, relaxed cooking and gathering room. Traditionally, the

Opposite: True to French Country style, this bedroom features a soothing, subdued color scheme with soft fabrics and an inviting chair.

Kitchen Recipes

Perhaps the most important room in the French-country home is the kitchen—not only a place for preparing meals, it has long been considered a family gathering spot and a place to share informal meals. Make your kitchen a little more welcoming by adding some of the following French Country touches.

◆ Tiles are an integral part of most French kitchens; in Provence, clay is plentiful and many kitchens showcase terra-cotta tiles. Keep in mind that the tile doesn't always need to be on the floor; try placing decorative ceramic or clay tiles on the wall above the stove.

◆ If your kitchen provides space for a dining table, consider adding one—preferably a simply styled wooden table. Often, French-country homes do not have separate dining rooms, so meals are taken in the kitchen; an intricately carved dining table might overpower this room, but a wooden table with clean lines will add just the right air of easy informality.

◆ Display your dishes! In America, it's common to have closed cabinetry above the kitchen counters, but a truly authentic French Country kitchen has open shelving, keeping items visible and within easy reach. If you have pottery, stoneware or china that you're particularly proud of, consider using a shelf or wire rack to exhibit your collection.

◆ Eliminate countertop and cabinet clutter by storing some items in hanging wire baskets.

◆ A center island is becoming a regular fixture in many American kitchens; to give it a French touch, try installing a pot and utensil rack overhead. If you favor copper cookware, hang your copper pots to create a definite French atmosphere.

◆ Start a kitchen garden. Fresh herbs are important to Provençal cuisine; popular ones are rosemary, fennel, sage and thyme. Fill your windowsill with small pots containing your favorite herbs.

French do not lay carpet, instead preferring hardwood or tiled floors accented by rugs of varying sizes. Fabric is everywhere, even on the walls—though wallpaper is used occasionally, the French much prefer to cover their walls with fabric. Slipcovers are widely admired; in addition to shielding the original fabric of the furniture from damage and offering easy cleaning, they make it simple to change the look of a room.

Soft, flowing fabrics, luxurious pillows and cushions, and soothing tones characterize Provençal bedrooms; though family living spaces are alive with color, the bedroom is a place of rest, and should therefore be more subdued. Like the main living areas, French Country bedrooms often feature several decorative rugs rather than wall-to-wall carpeting. Both canopied and four-poster beds, perfect for draping with a favorite fabric (perhaps muslin or one of the indiennes), are a popular choice and help to turn the room into a romantic, fairy-tale retreat. Keep in mind, though, that these two bed styles can look bulky when placed in a small or low-ceilinged bedroom. Linen and cotton are commonly chosen for bedding; cotton is affordable and easy to care for, while linen, though more costly and harder to maintain, becomes softer and stronger with use. French Country bedrooms often contain other furnish-

Opposite: Soft lighting, terra-cotta colored tiles and flowered wallpaper with an eye-catching border combine to give this dressing area a cozy air.

Festive shades of blue brighten this dining room, which showcases an intricately carved table and an aged chest-of-drawers topped by tall silver candlesticks.

Opposite: Wire baskets, a copper faucet and a unique selection of pottery establish the country character of this kitchen, decorated with the red, yellow and sage-green tones of Provence

ings such as chairs, chaise lounges or even writing desks, and the mix-and-match idea applies here as well.

Baths, though not quite as impressively styled as the rest of the home, still speak of a quiet luxury. Since many people see the bath as a place of relaxation, baths, like bedrooms, are often decorated with neutral tones. Though fine towels and washcloths are appreciated, the bath features much less fabric, and more wallpaper, than the rest of the home. Lighting is key—many European baths in urban areas are windowless, and must rely on artificial light. The French sometimes place wall sconces alongside the mirror, creating a gentle light for tasks like shaving and makeup application; also, skylights in the bath, highly popular in Europe, are being incorporated into American baths as well.

Little Saints:
THE SANTONS OF PROVENCE

The colorful village folk in this tableau depict one of the grand traditions of Provençal life: enjoying food and wine with friends.

The nativity scene, or *crèche*, has always been an important part of life in Provence. Originally inspired by St. Francis of Assisi, who in the 13th Century gathered people and animals in the forest to create living nativity scenes, the crèche became a beloved tradition, and an important part of Christmas celebrations; later, nativity figures were crafted from wood, glass, porcelain and tinted wax. By the 18th Century, many churches displayed large Nativity scenes with wooden figures dressed in fine clothing.

In 1789, during the French Revolution, churches were closed and people could no longer view the crèches during Mass. Jean-Louis Lagnel, an artist from Marseilles, began to fashion clay nativity figurines that the people of Provence could afford to place in their homes; these were called *santons*, or "little saints." Soon, he started to create figurines of local people such as shepherds, farmers and tradespeople; characters based on French folklore and traditions were also made, their brightly colored clothing painted on the clay. Nativity scenes filled with special, personalized santons became a part of Provençal homes.

More artists *(santonniers)* took up the trade, and each added new characters and hints of personal style. In 1803, a santon fair was held in Marseille, and artists viewed and learned from the work of others. Some changes were made; at first, santons were formed of unfired clay and were quite delicate; later, to make them more durable, they were fired in kilns. Another type of santon, called a dressed santon *(santon habilles)*, originated in 18th-Century Italy, but was quickly adapted to Provence. These figures, crafted from clay, were often a bit more detailed and wore clothing made from regional fabrics.

Today's santonniers have years of history and folklore to inspire their creations, and santons remain popular—the santon fair still goes on in Marseille, usually during the Christmas holidays. Many of the santons made today reflect a longing for the simpler times of the past, depicting tradespeople performing jobs that are no longer common. Santonniers often prefer to work their own clay, a long process that includes keeping the clay mixture in a cellar for more than a year. Research has also become part of the santonnier's job—today's little saints are greatly detailed, particularly the dressed santons, and artists want to make sure that their creations are historically accurate.

Right: Nativity santons were often gilded, to set them apart from those that depicted Provençal folk.

Opposite: A contented old couple strolls in this nostalgic scene.

Above: Two Provençal shepherds, one holding a lamb and the other carrying a lantern, come to pay their respects in this nativity scene.

Center: A lavender peddler wears a lacy shawl and traditional dress.

Food & Wine
THE PROVENÇAL TABLE

The gentle climate of Provence allows a wide variety of grapes to grow easily, making the area a good place to find lots of different wines.

Though Provence is not as famed for its wines as some other regions of France, its wine-making traditions are long-standing—Provence was actually the first region of France where grape vines were planted and cultivated, over two thousand years ago. The climate in Provence is perfect for growing grapes, which thrive in the hot, dry summers and mild winters. The mistral affects the vineyards; in fact, vines in some parts of Provence are planted at an angle, so the mistral will blow them straight eventually. The mountains of the Luberon protect the vineyards from sustaining too much wind damage.

France is known best for its red wines—the Cabernet Sauvignon of

Wine Facts

If you're not a wine connoisseur, you may be confused by some of the classifications that you see on wine labels. Here are explanations of the four categories of French wines:

◆ Wines given the designation *Appellation d'Origine Contrôéle* (AC) are held to the highest standards for production. The strict rules include what kinds of grapes can be grown, which methods are used for grape-picking, how much alcohol is in the wines, and how the wines are made. Often, these wines need to be bottled in the same region where they were produced.

◆ Wines labeled *Vin Délimité de Qualité Superiéure* (VDQS) are also subject to production rules, though their rules are less stern than the ones controlling AC wines.

◆ *Vin de Pays* translates to "country wine;" this denotes table wine that is identified by a particular area. Within this category, wines can be identified by one of four regions (the Loire Valley, the Southwest, the northern Rhône, or Provence), a department, or an individual winery. Though the rules are relaxed, they are strictly enforced for the smaller areas.

◆ *Vin de table*, the most basic classification, is simply table wine. Regulations overseeing the production of this wine are minimal.

Bordeaux, for example. Provence does produce red wine, and white as well, but the wine most associated with this Mediterreanean area is *vin rosé*, or rosé wine. This wine is made throughout France, but Provence serves as its biggest producer. Darker and spicier than a blush wine, rosé is a refreshing, warm-weather wine that complements the Provençal climate and cuisine.

Provençal wines go best with the cuisine, but there's also a vast array of before- and after-dinner drinks available—drinks consumed before dinner are called *apertifs*, and after-dinner drinks are known as *digestifs*. Perhaps the most famous apertif, immortalized in Peter Mayle's accounts

O, for a draught of vintage! that hath been
Cool'd a long age in the deep-delved earth,
Tasting of Flora and the country green,
Dance, and Provencal song, and sunburnt mirth!
 —*John Keats, "Ode to a Nightingale"*

of life in Provence, is pastis, a powerful drink made with aniseed, herbs and licorice steeped in alcohol. Pastis is reminiscent of an earlier drink—absinthe, also flavored with anise, which was popular in the 19th Century but was banned in France in the early 20th Century because of a hallucinogenic ingredient (wormwood). Today's pastis, though strong, does not contain wormwood and is quite legal. Other apertifs are white wine flavored with orange, red wine flavored with walnuts or blackberry liqueur, and another herbal drink, this one called *Suze*. Beverages consumed after a meal include *marc de Provence* (a strong brandy), more herbal liqueurs and sweet wines.

Food

The French are known for their enjoyment of life, and this is especially evident at the table. Food preparation is an artistic process, where careful planning and attentiveness to detail are paramount. A meal is an experience that should be savored, and the relaxed atmosphere of the Provençal countryside allows plenty of time to appreciate its cuisine.

Provençal cuisine is simple yet flavorful, with rich spices augmenting its soups, salads and entrees—it's also vastly different from what Americans are used to eating. The land in Provence, particularly in its mountainous areas, is not suitable for cattle grazing, so cows are scarce—consequently, beef and butter, along with certain kinds of cheese, are not

The Herbes de Provence—*usually a mix of savory, rosemary, marjoram, basil, oregano and thyme—offer a sampling of the spices commonly used in Provençal cooking.*

The Millionaire's Mushroom

If you hear the word "truffle" and think of a sweet chocolate treat, think again—in Provence, "truffle" refers to a fragrant, highly prized mushroom. Sometimes called Black Diamonds, truffles cannot be cultivated and only grow in certain soil conditions; most of them are found in Provence. From November to early March, truffle harvesters work with their specially trained dogs to find these mushrooms and take them to market. Due to demand, truffles are very expensive; most sellers will only accept cash payments, and transactions are conducted in private.

a major part of the Provençal diet. Goat cheese is plentiful, though—there are dozens of different varieties. Seafood also plays a large part in

the regional diet, especially in villages along the Mediterreanean coastline—Marseille is known for its *bouillabaisse*, a fish soup with garlic, saffron, pepper and other seasonings. Fresh vegetables are easily available; olives are common, and olive oil is the preferred cooking oil. Most foods are seasoned with the *Herbes de Provence*—savory, rosemary, marjoram, basil, oregano and thyme—in varying degrees, though other spices are used as well.

Provençal desserts vary, from fruit dishes to ice cream flavored with honey, from light, flaky pastries to fine chocolates. Candies are popular as well; in Aix-en-Provence, delicate almond candies called *calissons* prevail.

The regional diet of Provence is not only enjoyable—it is surprisingly healthy as well. Researchers have discovered that a Mediterranean-style diet—low-fat, with lots of fish, fruit and vegetables—can actually help to prevent heart disease and stroke.

Bottles of olive oil on display at a Provençal market; olive oil is preferred for cooking in the south of France.

PROVENÇAL
Style Showcase

DESIGN HPT22000I

Photography by Robert Bailey

A stucco finish, recessed balcony and spacious poolside terrace add the Mediterranean overtones of the Provençal coastline to this expansive estate home; corner quoins, a hipped roofline and gently arched windows add French styling. Double doors give entry to an interior that displays the best in modern floor planning, with plenty of space for both formal and informal gatherings. Fireplaces give warmth to the study, master suite and gathering room, while a quaint wood-burning pizza oven resides in the kitchen. French doors in the living room and master suite open to the terrace and pool area, offering a link to the outdoors. The pool house includes a fireplace, built-in shelves and a full bath.

The cozy and cheerful kitchen, highlighted by a charming tiled hearth, celebrates vivid colors and varied textures.

Opposite: An etched-glass, double-door entry, curved staircase and wrought-iron accents provide a dignified welcome in the foyer.

Stone supports for the veranda and pool house complement distinctive tiles and simple furnishings on the terrace.

Opposite: Elegant columns, gold accents and a luxurious tub make this a bath fit for royalty.

Upstairs, five suites—one that could serve as a private apartment or maid's quarters—share space with a bonus room. Three balconies, one accessible only from the bonus room, provide sweeping views of the living room, pool area and front property.

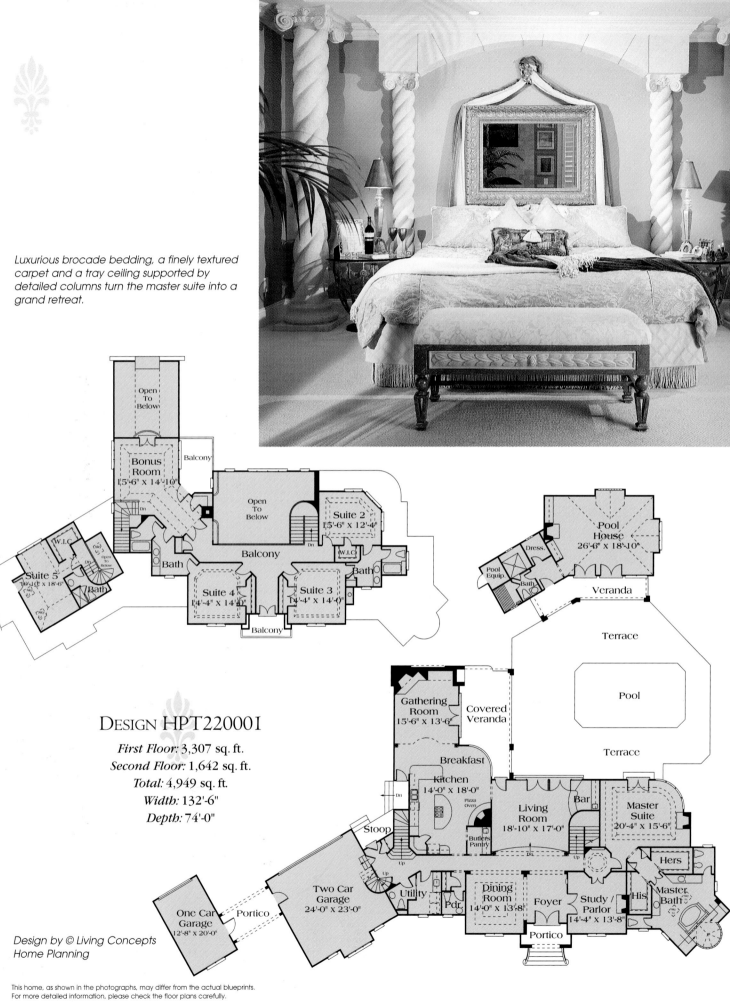

Luxurious brocade bedding, a finely textured carpet and a tray ceiling supported by detailed columns turn the master suite into a grand retreat.

DESIGN HPT220001

First Floor: 3,307 sq. ft.

Second Floor: 1,642 sq. ft.

Total: 4,949 sq. ft.

Width: 132'-6"

Depth: 74'-0"

Design by © Living Concepts Home Planning

This home, as shown in the photographs, may differ from the actual blueprints. For more detailed information, please check the floor plans carefully.

DESIGN HPT220002

This spacious French country estate displays a beautiful stone facade, gabled roof, multi-paned, arched casement windows with shutters, and stately stone chimneys. Double French doors open to reveal an interior that brings to life the rich textures and distinctive colors of Provençal

A soaring ceiling, large patterned rug and marble fireplace offer elegance in the grand room.

Photography by Robert Starling

living. A dormer window and a crystal and wrought-iron chandelier brighten the two-story foyer, which features a curving stairway with a hardwood balustrade.

Raised ceilings, archways, recessed lighting and hardwood floors characterize the first-floor living areas. The luxurious dining room is warmed by the glow of a cast-stone fireplace, flanked by built-in hutches with detailed molding. The study provides built-in bookcases, its own fireplace and access to the master suite. A nearby powder room accommodates guests and maintains privacy for the master suite.

In the grand room, a two-story beam ceiling enhances a wall of windows, which brings in plenty of natural light. Built-in bookcases flank a marble fireplace, and French doors lead to the rear terrace—a perfect arrangement for planned entertaining or cozy gatherings. A side staircase provides convenient access to the second-floor home theater. A well-organized kitchen features a food-prep island counter, walk-in pantry and plenty of cabinet space. Recessed lighting, dual sinks and tile counters provide an ideal cook-

White wicker and cool green hues define the sun room.

Opposite: A sweeping staircase, hardwood flooring and a wrought-iron chandelier provide a splendid introduction to this home.

ing area. A morning bay adjoins the kitchen and gathering room and offers views of the terrace. Detailed molding, built-in cabinetry, a fireplace and access to the terrace make the gathering room an inviting place for the family.

A lovely triple window highlights the master suite, which provides a morning kitchen and private access to the study. Separate walk-in closets and dressing areas allow privacy to the owners.

Tiled counters, wrought-iron accents and hardwood flooring bring a charmingly rustic look to this otherwise modern kitchen.

The spacious bath features a knee-space vanity, angled shower and a bumped-out tub with a bay window. Upstairs, each of the three bedroom suites has a walk-in closet and a private bath. Above the three-car garage, a full kitchen and bath make up a private apartment, perfect for a maid's quarters or live-in relatives.

Decorative tiles above the stove reflect the French Country spirit.

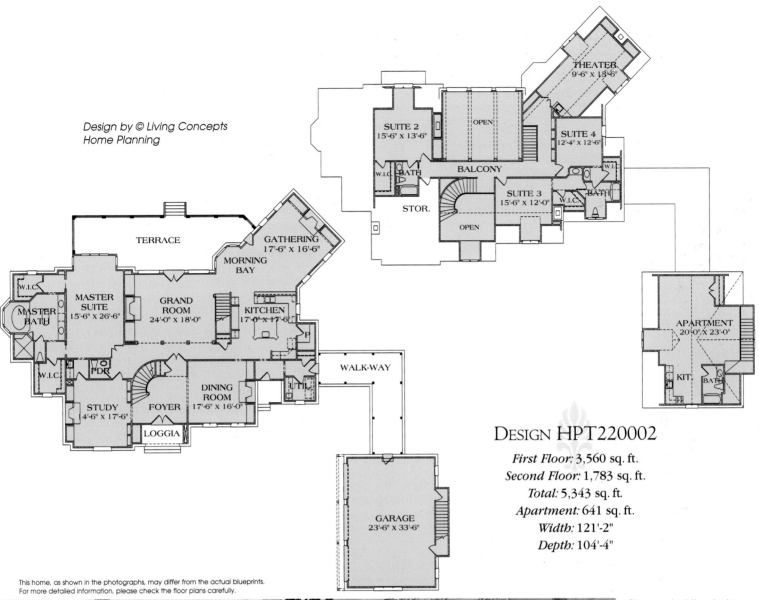

Design by © Living Concepts
Home Planning

TERRACE

GATHERING
17'-6" x 16'-6"

MORNING
BAY

W.I.C.

MASTER
SUITE
15'-6" x 26'-6"

GRAND
ROOM
24'-0" x 18'-0"

KITCHEN
17'-0" x 17'-6"

MASTER
BATH

P

W.I.C.

PDR

STUDY
4'-6" x 17'-6"

FOYER

DINING
ROOM
17'-6" x 16'-0"

UTIL

WALK-WAY

LOGGIA

SUITE 2
15'-6" x 13'-6"

OPEN

SUITE 4
12'-4" x 12'-6"

THEATER
9'-6" x 18'-6"

W.I.C.

BATH

BALCONY

W.I.

STOR.

SUITE 3
15'-6" x 12'-0"

W.I.C.

BATH

OPEN

APARTMENT
20'-0" x 23'-0"

KIT.

BATH

GARAGE
23'-6" x 33'-6"

DESIGN HPT220002

First Floor: 3,560 sq. ft.

Second Floor: 1,783 sq. ft.

Total: 5,343 sq. ft.

Apartment: 641 sq. ft.

Width: 121'-2"

Depth: 104'-4"

This home, as shown in the photographs, may differ from the actual blueprints.
For more detailed information, please check the floor plans carefully.

Blue-and-white chairs
and a simple wooden
table give a fresh
country look to the
dining room.

A fireplace topped by tall candlesticks adds extra warmth to this living room to balance the cool green walls, while a unique mix of furnishings draws the eye.

DESIGN HPT220003

High-pitched roofs, divided-light windows and delicate arches hint at the historical roots of this modern French-style estate. 17th-Century French architecture, influenced by the Renaissance, took a quiet turn toward a more artistic, less ornate, elevation. The interior steps out in 21st-Century style. A two-story foyer introduces the home, and is flanked by the formal dining room and a den that can double as a guest suite. The central gathering room, enhanced by a fireplace, built-in cabinets and shelves, and access to the rear veranda, is open to both the kitchen and the morning room. The kitchen provides a work island, two stoves and wide wrapping counters, while the morning room enjoys natural light from windows on two of its three walls.

Gently rounded dormers, arched windows and stone accents create a French Country facade for this home.

A second fireplace is the focal point of the den, where a rich shade of red blends with green and gold for a regal look.

The master suite, set to the right of the first floor and accessed by double doors, offers plenty of amenities—private entry to the veranda, a walk-in closet, and a spacious bath with dual vanities, raised oval tub, separate shower and compartmented toilet. Family sleeping quarters are found on the second floor: two bedrooms, one with a walk-in closet, share a full bath. A lengthy hallway and a cozy loft area provide a grand view of the gathering room. The plan is complete with a large bonus room above the garage.

This kitchen's tiled floor is accented by decorative tiles and a pottery display shelf above the stove.

Highlights of the rear elevation include a high steep roofline and two stone chimneys; a wide veranda provides outdoor living space.

Design by © Living Concepts
Home Planning

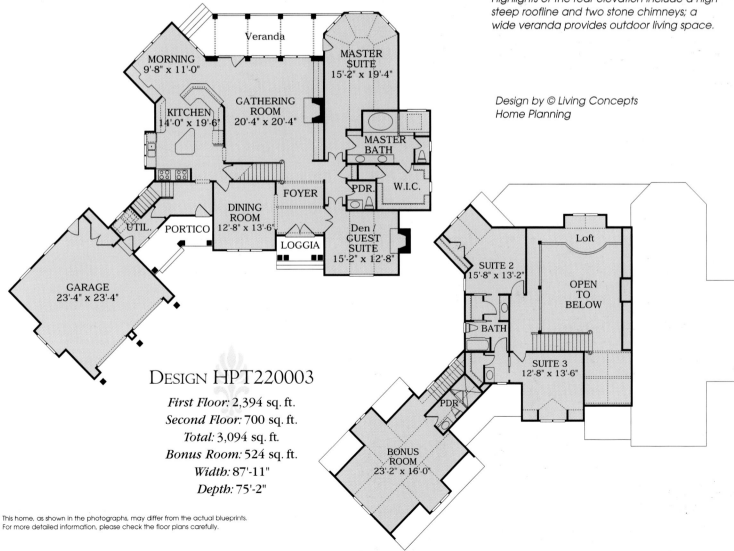

DESIGN HPT220003

First Floor: 2,394 sq. ft.
Second Floor: 700 sq. ft.
Total: 3,094 sq. ft.
Bonus Room: 524 sq. ft.
Width: 87'-11"
Depth: 75'-2"

This home, as shown in the photographs, may differ from the actual blueprints.
For more detailed information, please check the floor plans carefully.

DESIGN HPT220004

Inspired by the architecture of the French countryside, this design incorporates state-of-the-art technology with a centuries-old style. A stone-and-brick façade creates an intentionally aged look that is a perfect complement to the high-tech intercom and security systems with video monitoring, thermal double-glazed windows, and energy-efficient heating and cooling throughout the home. The time-honored tone of this house is punctuated inside by a satisfying combination of antique and contemporary furniture.

Crosscut travertine floors, arched stacked-stone walls and a winding wrought-iron staircase give the spacious foyer an Old World flavor. The wide foyer opens to both the formal dining room and central great room. This free-flowing design allows an impressive style of entertaining, whether formal or casual. In the dining room,

An enchanting staircase highlights the foyer and leads up to a spacious media room.

Photography by B. Massey Photographers

A brick exterior, accented by stones, sports tall arched windows and a flower box.

fabric-draped walls, a gold-leafed ceiling and a unique octagonal table create a formal yet intimate setting for any occasion. The great room provides a graceful arched entry from the main hallway and access to the rear covered porch. A stone fireplace is the striking centerpiece of this room and is flanked by arched built-ins. A wrought-iron gate guards the entry to the lovely wine niche, where a hand-painted fresco stimulates the imagination.

The custom-designed gourmet kitchen includes a stainless-steel range, hood and warming shelves, a silent dishwasher, double ovens and a remote ventilator. Distressed brick flooring, a fireplace and an exposed-beam ceiling complete the fabulous charm of this culinary paradise. The breakfast area includes floor-to-ceiling windows that add light and bring a sense of the countryside indoors. Nearby, a keeping room features an impressive stone fireplace that imparts a medieval flavor to the room.

An appreciation of style, space and design is showcased in the dramatic master suite, complete with a fireplace, sitting area and lavishly draped windows. Tall windows frame the hearth, and a

A stone hearth warms the keep-ing room, enhanced by plenty of natural light.

door leads out to a private area of the rear porch. The luxurious bath provides a sheered-silk ceiling and soft color palette, two walk-in closets, separate vanities and a sunken tub.

On the second floor, a gallery overlooking the foyer leads to the family's sleeping quarters. Each of the secondary bedrooms has separate access to a full bath and plenty of wardrobe space. A bonus room offers the possibility of a computer nook, home office or play room. At the opposite corner of the second floor, the media room has been customized with a state-of-the-art entertainment center that includes surround sound.

A creative landscape package with a centrally controlled irrigation system and site lighting will be the envy of your neighborhood, even if you live in the French countryside. This home is designed with a walkout basement foundation.

A media room includes built-ins and easily converts to a study or den.

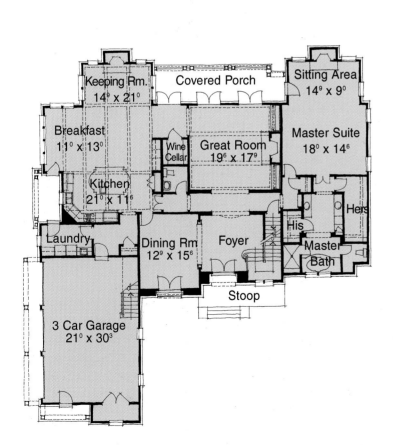

Keeping Rm.
14⁹ x 21⁰

Covered Porch

Sitting Area
14⁹ x 9⁰

Breakfast
11⁰ x 13⁰

Wine Cellar

Great Room
19⁶ x 17⁹

Master Suite
18⁰ x 14⁶

Kitchen
21⁰ x 11⁶

Laundry

Dining Rm
12⁹ x 15⁶

Foyer

His

Hers

Master Bath

Stoop

3 Car Garage
21⁰ x 30³

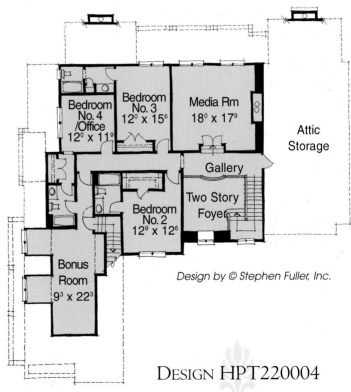

Bedroom No. 4 /Office
12⁰ x 11⁹

Bedroom No. 3
12⁰ x 15⁶

Media Rm
18⁰ x 17⁹

Attic Storage

Gallery

Bonus Room
9³ x 22³

Bedroom No. 2
12⁹ x 12⁶

Two Story Foyer

Design by © Stephen Fuller, Inc.

DESIGN HPT220004

First Floor: 2,963 sq. ft.
Second Floor: 1,308 sq. ft.
Total: 4,271 sq. ft.
Bonus Room: 358 sq. ft.
Width: 72'-0"
Depth: 76'-6"

This home, as shown in the photographs, may differ from the actual blueprints.
For more detailed information, please check the floor plans carefully.

Alan Mascord Design Associates, Inc.
Founded in 1983 as a local supplier to the building community, Mascord Design Associates of Portland, Oregon began to successfully publish plans nationally in 1985. The company's trademark is creating floor plans that work well and exhibit excellent traffic patterns.

Design Basics, Inc.
For nearly a decade, Design Basics, a nationally recognized home design service located in Omaha, has been developing plans for custom home builders. Since 1987, the firm has consistently appeared in *Builder* magazine, the official magazine of the National Association of Home Builders, as one of the top-selling designers.

Donald A. Gardner Architects
The South Carolina firm of Donald A. Gardner was established in response to a growing demand for residential designs that reflect constantly changing lifestyles. The company's specialty is providing homes with refined, custom-style details and unique features such as passive-solar designs and open floor plans.

Fillmore Design Group
Fillmore Design Group was formed in 1960 in Oklahoma City by Robert L. Fillmore, president and founder. "Our designs are often characterized by their European influence, by massive brick gables and by high-flowing, graceful rooflines," comments Fillmore.

Home Design Services
Home Design Services is a full-service design firm that has specialized in residential and multi-family design for thirty years. The firm offers a full complement of services, taking a project from concept through completed construction documents. The company's vast experience provides a considerable knowledge of current design trends.

Home Planners
Headquartered in Tucson, Arizona, with additional offices in Detroit, Home Planners is one of the longest-running and most successful home design firms in the United States. With over 2,500 designs in its portfolio, the company provides a wide range of styles, sizes and types of homes for the residential builder.

Larry E. Belk Designs
Through the years, Larry E. Belk has worked with individuals and builders alike to provide a quality product. Flowing, open spaces and interesting angles define his interiors. Great emphasis is placed on providing views that showcase the natural environment.

Living Concepts Home Planning
With more than twenty years of design experience, Living Concepts Home Planning has built an outstanding reputation for its many award-winning residential designs. Based in Charlotte, North Carolina, the company was founded by partners Frank Snodgrass, Chris Boush, Kim Bunting and Derik Boush. Because of its affinity for glass and design that take full advantage of outside views, Living Concepts specializes in homes for golf and lakefront communities.

Select Home Designs
Select Home Designs has 50 years of experience delivering top-quality and affordable residential designs to the North American housing market. Since the company's inception in 1948, more than 350,000 new homes throughout North America and overseas have been built from Select's plans. Select's design team is constantly striving to develop the best new plans for today's lifestyles.

The Sater Design Collection Inc.
The Sater Design Collection has a long established tradition of providing South Florida's most diverse and extraordinary custom designed homes. This is exemplified by over 50 national design awards, numerous magazine features and, most important, satisfied clients.

Stephen Fuller, Inc.
Stephen S. Fuller established his design group with the tenets of innovation, quality, originality and uncompromising architectural techniques in traditional and European homes. Especially popular throughout the Southeast, Stephen Fuller's plans are known for their extensive detail and thoughtful design.

Ahmann Design, Inc.
Ahmann Design is a residential design firm specializing in custom residential, stock plan sales, and color rendering. Recognized several times as a finalist in *Professional Builder* Magazine's "Best of American Living" contest, Ahmann Design, Inc. continues to grow as a leader in the residential design market.

Greg Marquis and Associates
Incorporating the various features of Southern architecture, the designs of Greg Marquis include emphsis on accurate, detailed drawings and functional floor plans. Greg's designs focus on utilizing space without sacrificing the unique and appealing floor plans which have made his designs so popular.

Breland & Farmer
Designer Edsel Breland is owner and president of Breland & Farmer Designers, Inc., which he founded in 1973. The homes designed by Breland have a definite Southern signature, but fit perfectly in any region.

Drummond Designs
Drummond Designs has been involved in the business of residential architecture since 1973, with over 70,000 satisfied customers. Their primary goal is to offer consumers top-quality homes that meet or exceed most of the world's building code requirements.

Frank Betz Associates, Inc.
Frank Betz Associates, Inc., located in Smyrna, Georgia, is one of the nation's leaders in the design of stock plans. FBA, Inc. has provided builders and developers with home plans since 1977.

Nelson Design Group
Michael E. Nelson is a certified member of the American Institute of Building Designers, providing both custom and stock residential home plans. He designs homes that families enjoy now and which also bring maximum appraisal value at resale.

The Housing Associates
Rodney L. Pfotenhauer opened the doors of The Housing Associates in 1987 as a design consultant and illustrator for the manufactured housing industry. Pfotenhauer's designs are characterized by carefully composed traditional exteriors with up-to-date interiors.

Archival Designs, Inc.
David Marc Loftus of Archival Designs, Inc. has celebrated fifteen years in the residential design business. His firm has been growing at an accelerated rate because his designs reflect the collective wisdom of the past. His award-winning style is called "Classic Traditional."

Andy McDonald Design Group
Andy McDonald, CPBD, is a residential designer whose scrupulous regard for scale, balance and historical detailing has earned him a stellar reputation. As a result of his national recognition, Andy has been commissioned to design entire communities, as well as style-coordinated parcels in upscale developments. Of particular appeal to McDonald are the classic designs of Old World France, Spain and England.

American Traditions
American Traditions is a design firm totally committed to the various styles known collectively as the American home. The earliest significant influences came straight from the countries of Europe and the homes of our forefathers. American Traditions stays true to those influences but adds what they call the "American snap"—the upbeat look of new construction and light-filled floor plans.

COZY COTTAGES

"Every man has two nations, and one of them is France."
—Benjamin Franklin
Scientist, inventor, statesman
Ambassador to France
1706-1790

Design HPT220005

First Floor: 1,196 sq. ft.
Second Floor: 934 sq. ft.
Total: 2,130 sq. ft.
Width: 40'-0"
Depth: 30'-0"

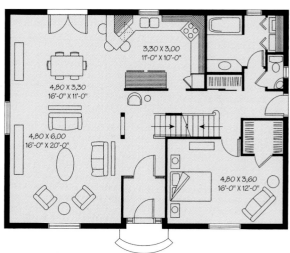

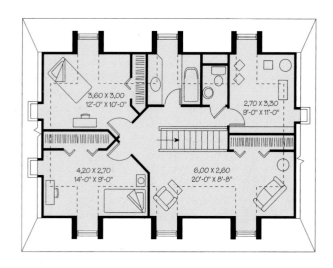

Quaint French cottage style creates a sumptuous floor plan perfect for any family. Stucco, corner quoins, French shutters and a shingled roof are of notable European influence, while the front dormers possess a countryside simplicity. A petite welcoming porch introduces you to the front door. To the left, the family room is open to the formal dining room. Double doors from the dining room open to the rear of the home. The adjoining island countertop kitchen features a breakfast bar. Down the hall, the first-floor master suite—secluded for extra privacy—features a walk-in closet. Across the hall, a huge bath resides next to a separate compartmented toilet. Upstairs, a huge loft area makes a perfect media room and is illuminated by two front-facing dormers. Two family bedrooms share the hall bath that includes a separate compartmented toilet. The third room on the second floor can be used as a study room, playroom or fourth bedroom. This home is designed with a basement foundation.

Design HPT220006

Square Footage: 1,153
Width: 36'-0"
Depth: 34'-0"

3,00 X 3,60
10'-0" X 12'-0"

2,90 X 3,60
9'-8" X 12'-0"

3,60 X 3,60
12'-0" X 12'-0"

4,10 X 4,90
13'-8" X 16'-4"

3,00 X 3,40
10'-0" X 11'-4"

This petite cottage home is alive with European romance. The brick and stucco exterior is topped by a red shingled roof and is illuminated by graceful arching windows. Classic columns elegantly frame the front-door entrance. The entryway offers a coat closet and is spacious enough for a plant and chair. Double doors open into the home. The one-story elevation is perfect for a retired couple or small families looking to avoid the daily hassle of going up and down stairs. To the left, the formal living room is perfect for elegant or casual entertaining. The U-shaped kitchen overlooks a breakfast bar to the eating area. Both rooms provide views to the backyard. The master bedroom also provides a beautiful view of the backyard and features a large closet space. Down the hall, a smaller guest suite offers a smaller closet space. Both rooms share a full hall bath between them that provides a whirlpool tub and separate shower. This home is designed with a basement foundation.

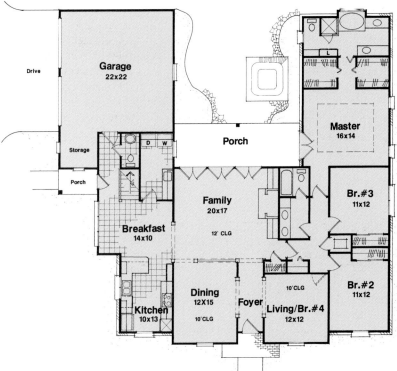

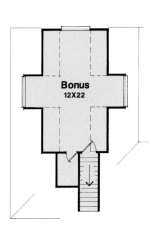

DESIGN HPT220007

Square Footage: 2,215
Bonus Room: 253 sq. ft.
Width: 63'-0"
Depth: 61'-0"

Luxurious French style and European elegance combine to create a simple facade with an abundance of arches and exterior materials. This symmetrical cottage design offers single-story convenience with an optional bonus room over the garage—great for a home office! Inside, the formal living room could also be used as a fourth bedroom. The columned dining room opens into a spacious family room with a fireplace and built-in shelves, plus a nice view of the rear porch through a series of French doors. The master suite also accesses the rear porch and features a tray ceiling, twin walk-in closets and separate lavatories in the whirlpool master bath. Two family bedrooms share a full hall bath. On the opposite side of the home, the tiled kitchen and breakfast area create an informal place for family meals. A large laundry room with a built-in sink makes chores easier. Extra storage space is available in the garage.

This charming cottage home possesses a heart of gold with French folk style. A quartet of blended materials offers an ethereal elevation perfect for everyday living or a vacation retreat. An arched stone entrance welcomes you inside beyond the front porch. Wide views invite natural light and provide a sense of spaciousness in the living room. A fireplace with an extended hearth is framed by built-in bookcases and complemented by a sloped ceiling. A well-organized kitchen provides wrapping counters and a serving ledge, which overlooks the breakfast area. Bright light fills this casual dining space through a wide window. The formal dining room is highlighted by a coffered ceiling and enjoys easy service from the kitchen through a lovely set of double doors. The master suite features a private bath with a garden tub and a separate shower with a seat. Two additional family bedrooms share a full hall bath. A two-car garage with extra storage space and a useful utility room complete this one-story design. Please specify crawlspace or slab foundation when ordering.

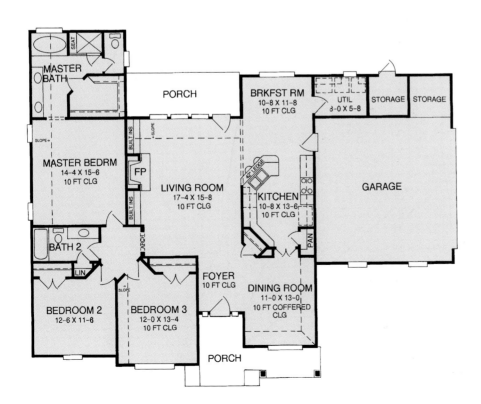

DESIGN HPT220008

Square Footage: 1,890
Width: 65'-10"
Depth: 53'-5"

Design HPT220009

First Floor: 820 sq. ft.
Second Floor: 1,040 sq. ft.
Total: 1,860 sq. ft.
Width: 33'-0"
Depth: 36'-0"

This miniature version of the grand manors found in Europe boasts an abundance of amenities and gains a great deal in efficiencies within. With a townhouse silhouette, the architecture reflects French and Victorian influences found in its brick and stucco exterior. The main level offers a foyer with a hall closet and a charming family room warmed by a fireplace to the right. The gourmet kitchen, large enough for a breakfast table, is open to the more formal dining room. A laundry and powder room are tucked away behind the garage, which is thoughtfully placed near the kitchen. Bedrooms are located on the upper level. A spacious and pampering master suite features a private whirlpool bath, a walk-in closet and double doors to a petite balcony overlooking the front yard. Two additional family bedrooms on the upper level share a bath that includes a shower between them. This home is designed with a basement foundation.

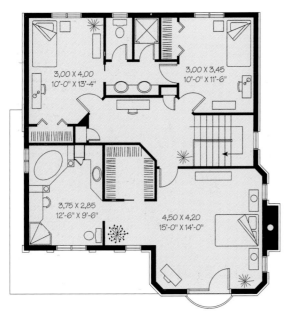

Design HPT220010

First Floor: 676 sq. ft.

Second Floor: 686 sq. ft.

Total: 1,362 sq. ft.

Width: 26'-0"

Depth: 26'-0"

This French townhouse offers enchanting European curvatures and a dramatic yet compact two-story elevation. Beautiful arching windows sweep the facade with breathtaking elegance. The front, second-story windows outside of the family bedrooms boast decorative plant ledges. A quaint front porch introduces you into the formal foyer that offers a hall coat closet. To the left, a door opens into the formal living room. This room connects to the formal dining room to the rear. The kitchen is large enough for a family breakfast table and easily serves the dining room—a corner pantry is located nearby. A first-floor powder room resides next to a side outdoor access. Up the stairs, the master bedroom features large closet space and views of the backyard. Two other family bedrooms, overlook the front yard. These three family bedrooms share a hall linen closet and a hall bath that includes a corner tub, a separate shower and a towel closet. This home is designed with a basement foundation.

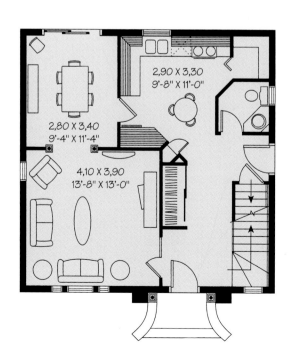

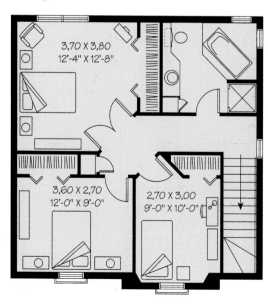

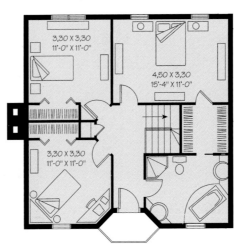

Design HPT220011

First Floor: 1,078 sq. ft.

Second Floor: 772 sq. ft.

Total: 1,850 sq. ft.

Width: 36'-0"

Depth: 34'-0"

This French cottage is well placed on the countryside scene. Stucco and stone and French shutters combine to give this home a distinctly European appearance. A petite portico makes a welcoming first impression. Inside the foyer, a full bath is found to the right. To the left, a quiet home office is reserved for the workaholic of the family. Straight ahead, the living room is warmed by a stone fireplace and is open to the dining area. A wall of windows at the rear of the home provides backyard views from both the living and dining rooms. Double doors open into the kitchen, which boasts plenty of counter space and is large enough to hold a breakfast table. The kitchen provides access to a side porch, located behind the two-car garage. A second front entrance is placed between the garage and laundry room. Its foyer features a coat closet. Upstairs, the master bedroom offers a walk-through closet with private access to the hall bath. The bathroom features corner tub, separate shower and double vanities. Two other family bedrooms each offer closet space. The hallway accesses a petite second-floor porch overlooking the front yard. This home is designed with a basement foundation.

DESIGN HPT220012

First Floor: 1,346 sq. ft.
Second Floor: 1,320 sq. ft.
Total: 2,666 sq. ft.
Width: 44'-0"
Depth: 30'-0"

A stone facade and classical symmetry shape the exterior of this lovely European cottage. Steps lead up to a charming front entrance. The entranceway makes way for a foyer with a coat closet. A professional home office is located to the right. To the left of the foyer, a warming fireplace is set between the open living and dining rooms—perfect for formal entertaining or casual family occasions. The gourmet country kitchen boasts an abundance of counter space. A petite powder room and laundry facilities complete the first floor. Upstairs, the master suite overlooks the front yard. It boasts a roomy sitting area and a private fireplace. Closet space extends into the private master bath, which offers a luxury corner tub and two separate vanities. A separate shower stall is placed between the family hall bath and the master bath. The two family bedrooms overlook the backyard and share the nearby full hall bath. This home is designed with a basement foundation.

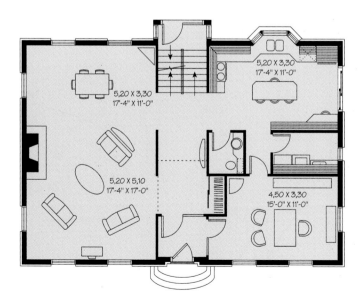

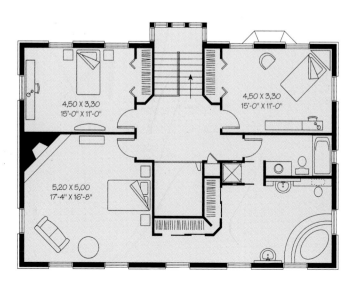

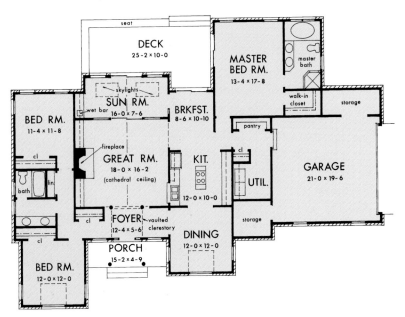

DESIGN HPT220013

Square Footage: 2,099
Width: 72'-6"
Depth: 53'-10"

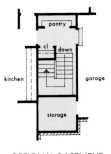

OPTIONAL BASEMENT
STAIR LOCATION

REAR VIEW

This enchanting design incorporates the best in floor planning all on one amenity-filled level. Large arched windows and corner quoins lend a distinctly European flavor to the feeling of this brick-exterior home. A front porch framed by columns welcomes you inside to an inviting foyer. The central great room is the hub of the plan, from which all other rooms radiate. It is highlighted with a fireplace and cathedral ceiling. Nearby is a skylit sun room with sliding glass doors to the rear deck and a built-in wet bar. The galley-style kitchen adjoins an attached breakfast room. The master suite is split from the family bedrooms and accesses the rear deck. The pampering master bath offers a whirlpool tub, separate shower and twin vanities. Family bedrooms on the opposite side of the house share a full hall bath. Extra storage space can be found in the two-car garage.

DESIGN HPT220014

Square Footage: 1,576
Width: 60'-6"
Depth: 50'-9"

This stately, three-bedroom, one-story home exhibits sheer elegance with its large, arched windows, corner quoins, round columns, covered porch and brick veneer. In the foyer, natural light enters through arched windows in clerestory dormers. The European-style silhouette is interrupted by country dormers overlooking the front yard—this detail lends a more cottage feel to the overall plan. A formal front porch, flanked by columns, welcomes you into the entry foyer. In the great room, a dramatic cathedral ceiling and a fireplace set the mood. Through gracious, round columns, the kitchen and breakfast rooms open up. The breakfast room overlooks an enormous rear deck with a sizzling spa—perfect for outdoor entertaining and weekend relaxation. For sleeping, turn to the master bedroom. Here, a large walk-in closet and a well-planned master bath with a double-bowl vanity, garden tub and shower will pamper. Two additional bedrooms are located at the opposite end of the house for privacy.

Design HPT220015

Square Footage: 1,890
Width: 40'-0"
Depth: 73'-4"

It's easy to imagine this charming one-story home nestled in the picturesque and romantic countryside of France. However, this amenity-filled plan—designed to fit easily on a narrow lot—is perfectly suited to any neighborhood wherever you live. Efficient floor planning places the kitchen and morning room to the left of the foyer, which allows the formal dining room, the great room and the master bedroom to take advantage of rear views. The open dining room will be warmed by the fireplace from the nearby great room. The rear deck is perfect for outdoor entertaining. From the garage—cleverly disguised as a barn—there is a laundry room adjoining two secondary bedrooms and a bath. The master bedroom is highlighted by a dressing area with a walk-in closet and a master bath with a whirlpool tub, a double-bowl vanity and a separate shower. A stairway leads to a large attic storage area, which can be modified for future development if needed.

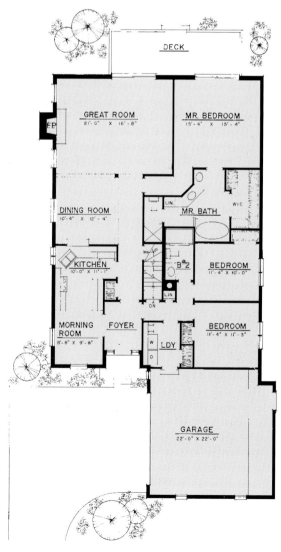

DESIGN HPT220016

First Floor: 1,277 sq. ft.

Second Floor: 378 sq. ft.

Total: 1,655 sq. ft.

Width: 74'-8"

Depth: 42'-8"

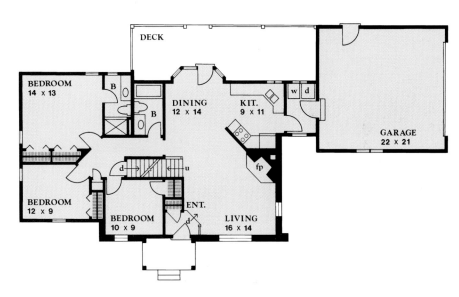

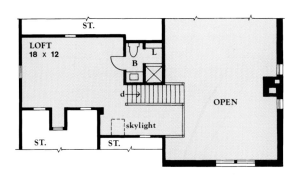

Graceful, curving eaves and a spectacular arched window give this stucco-and-stone home its distinctive elegance. While the exterior of this home offers abundant Old World charm, the interior is filled with contemporary amenities. A petite front porch welcomes you inside. From the entrance, an expansive open area comprised of the living room, dining room and kitchen—all with beamed ceilings—provides a dramatic centerpiece to the overall plan. The enormous arched window illuminates the interior. The angled bay window from the dining room opens conveniently to the rear deck, furnishing options for dining alfresco. Sleeping quarters located on the left wing of the first floor include a master bedroom with a private bath and closet space. A full hall bath serves both family bedrooms and is readily accessible to guests. Upstairs, a spacious loft is illuminated by a skylight and provides its own bathroom and a balcony overlooking the living room.

DESIGN HPT220017

Square Footage: 2,598
Width: 68'-3"
Depth: 78'-3"

The overall design of this home is reminiscent of a European country cottage. French accents are highlighted inside and out. Stucco and stone create a fairy tale ambiance on the exterior, while amenities enhance the interior. From the arched double-door entry, columns add a stately elegance to the foyer and to the exquisite great room with its warming fireplace. A wall of French doors accesses the rear deck from the dining and great rooms and illuminates interior spaces. The formal dining room connects to the L-shaped kitchen. A bayed breakfast nook opens to a wonderful keeping room with outdoor access and a fireplace. A large utility room separates two family bedrooms and their shared bath from the master suite. The bayed master bedroom suite features a beautiful coffered ceiling and a luxurious bath with a walk-in closet, separate sinks and a corner tub. This home is designed with a walkout basement foundation.

Bedroom
#3
11⁶ x 11⁰

Bedroom
#2
11³ x 11⁰

Porch

Breakfast
10⁰ x 9⁰

Kitchen
12⁰ x13³

Sun Room
12⁰ x 13⁹

Porch

Great
Room
18⁰ x 14⁰

Master
Bedroom
13³ x 15⁶

Dining
Room
10⁷ x 10⁷

Two Car
Garage
20⁸ x 21⁸

Den/
Guest Room
13⁴ x 14⁸

Design HPT220018

Square Footage: 2,140
Width: 62'-0"
Depth: 60'-6"

A blend of stucco and stone creates the exterior charm of this Country French home. French shutters accent the picturesque windows. Inside, the great room offers a focal-point fireplace for cozy occasions. The large, neighboring dining room enjoys a beautiful triple window combination. Adjacent to the foyer is a den with a built-in window seat and a warming hearth. This room can double as a guest bedroom. The kitchen in this home is centrally located and offers an island workstation. This efficient planning offers views into both the breakfast room and sun room, with access to the covered rear porch. Two bedrooms to the left rear of the home, with a shared bath and double vanity, are perfectly situated on the opposite side of the home from the private master suite. The master suite is a quiet retreat, offering a whirlpool bath and walk-in closet. This home is designed with a walkout basement foundation.

Design HPT220019

Square Footage: 1,807
Width: 74'-0"
Depth: 44'-0"

The striking European facade of this home includes a beautiful stone exterior, complete with stone quoins, a shingled rooftop and French-style shutters on the front windows. Rounded arched windows add to the authentic European and antique feeling of this design. Step inside to the tiled entrance gallery and through to the great room enhanced by a ten-foot ceiling and an indulging fireplace. A large island in the kitchen provides plenty of much-needed counter space for the gourmet of the family. The great room and tiled dining room overlook a rear patio. An element of privacy has been observed with the master suite, which is separated from the other two bedrooms. The suite includes a lavish master bath, walk-in closet and private outdoor patio. The two other family bedrooms share a full bath between them. An oversized two-car garage, a useful utility room and the covered patio are just some of the added amenities.

Design HPT220020

Square Footage: 2,282
Width: 63'-10"
Depth: 71'-1"

The French ambiance of refined Europe combined with country coziness suggest the creation of a petite family palace, complete with a brick and stone silhouette. The stone entranceway and steep rooflines accent the rustic nature of this home's facade. French doors lead guests and homeowners into an elegant tiled entryway and gallery. This home offers plenty of living space throughout. The enchanting living and dining rooms are available for formal occasions. The large angled kitchen, featuring an island, extends into the open breakfast nook. A fireplace warms the family room in the winter and offers access to a covered rear patio for convenient summer outdoor entertaining. Another covered patio can be privately accessed through the master suite and breakfast nook. The master suite pampers the homeowner with a lavish bath and enormous walk-in closet. A second bedroom is located nearby and includes a walk-in closet. Bedrooms 3 and 4 are located on the opposite side of the home and share a full hall bath. A utility room and a three-car garage make this design complete.

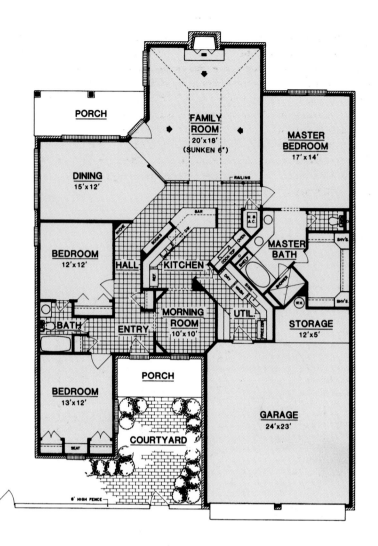

PORCH

FAMILY
ROOM
20'x18'
(SUNKEN 6')

MASTER
BEDROOM
17'x14'

DINING
15'x12'

RAILING

BAR

K &
AC

BEDROOM
12'x12'

HALL

KITCHEN

MASTER
BATH

SHV'S

BATH

ENTRY

MORNING
ROOM
10'x10'

UTIL

STORAGE
12'x5'

SHV'S

BEDROOM
13'x12'

PORCH

SEAT

COURTYARD

GARAGE
24'x23'

8' HIGH FENCE

DESIGN HPT220021

Square Footage: 1,994
Width: 49'-0"
Depth: 68'-0"

French accents inspire this European-influenced creation. A quaint courtyard, reminiscent of the Old World, introduces guests into this family home compound. Inside the tiled entrance, the kitchen is central and is open to the morning room—perfect for casual family gatherings. A sunken family room with sloped ceilings features a fireplace and access to the rear porch. This room also connects to the formal dining room, conveniently across the way from the kitchen for easy service. The right side of the plan offers the master bedroom, with a private whirlpool bath and enormous walk-in closet. Two additional family bedrooms reside on the left side of the plan. They share access to a full hall bath, across from the entryway. A two-car garage and a useful utility room complete this home. Please specify crawlspace or slab foundation when ordering.

DESIGN HPT220022

Square Footage: 1,434
Width: 70'-0"
Depth: 44'-0"

With French countryside elegance, this grand facade contains a petite interior that's perfect for a romantic hideaway on the Riviera. Gracefully arched windows illuminate the home and European-style corner quoins create a stunning first impression. The alluring floor plan of this three-bedroom home offers many charming amenities. The spacious master suite possesses a quaint master bath and a walk-in closet. Two additional family bedrooms share access to a full hall bath. The open living areas feature ten-foot ceilings, which add to a lofty sense of spaciousness. The living room is open to porches via French doors at the front and rear of the plan—a fireplace warms the living room on cool evenings. The cottage-style kitchen offers a dinette for casual occasions, while the dining room is reserved for more formal engagements. A two-car garage with extra storage completes this one-story home. Please specify crawlspace or slab foundation when ordering.

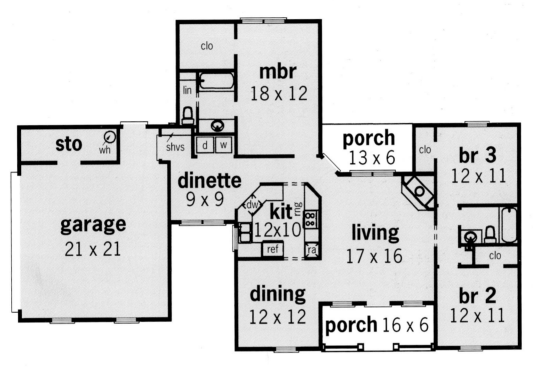

DESIGN HPT220023

Square Footage: 2,200
Width: 56'-0"
Depth: 74'-0"

The magic and romance of the European-style cottage is echoed in the silhouette of this tantalizing design. French accents and stucco styling enhance the exterior, while beautiful amenities reign free within the interior. A versatile swing room is a highlight of this compact and charming French-style home. Using the optional door off the entry, the swing room makes a perfect office, or it can be used as a bedroom or study. The king-sized master suite is isolated for privacy and offers a spacious pampering bath and walk-in closet with passage to the utility room. The open and spacious living room features lofty twelve-foot ceilings, as well as built-ins and a quaint fireplace. The gourmet kitchen is conveniently set between the family eating area and the formal dining room. The rear porch is the perfect addition for outdoor entertainment. Two secondary bedrooms offer walk-in closets and private baths. Please specify crawlspace or slab foundation when ordering.

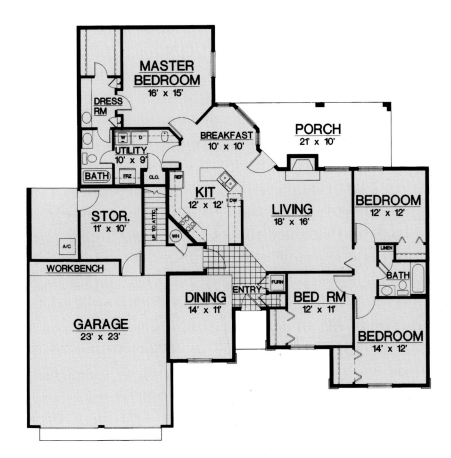

Design HPT220024

Square Footage: 1,828
Width: 64'-0"
Depth: 62'-0"

With hipped roofs and muntin windows, this attractive facade brings curb appeal to this European-style home. Stucco, corner quoins and arching accents create a breathtaking blend. Inside, the dining room sits just left of the tiled entry, while the kitchen resides to the left of the living room with a fireplace. The spacious kitchen features an angled-counter, which overlooks the bayed breakfast room and leads to the utility room. The doorway between the breakfast room and great room opens to the rear porch—perfect for outdoor grilling. The master bedroom contains a vast walk-in closet, a vanity with a sink in the dressing room and a full bath. Three bedrooms occupy the right side of the home and share a full bath and a linen closet. The two-car garage holds a roomy storage area and access to a side exit. Please specify basement, crawlspace or slab foundation when ordering.

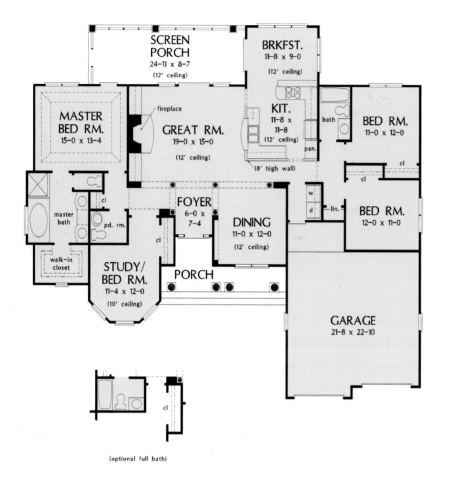

SCREEN PORCH
24-11 x 8-7
(12' ceiling)

BRKFST.
11-8 x 9-0
(12' ceiling)

MASTER BED RM.
15-0 x 13-4

fireplace

GREAT RM.
19-0 x 15-0
(12' ceiling)

KIT.
11-8 x 11-8
(12' ceiling)

bath

BED RM.
11-0 x 12-0

pan.

(8' high wall)

master bath

cl

pd. rm.

FOYER
6-0 x 7-4

cl

w

d

lin.

cl

cl

BED RM.
12-0 x 11-0

walk-in closet

DINING
11-0 x 12-0
(12' ceiling)

STUDY/ BED RM.
11-4 x 12-0
(10' ceiling)

PORCH

GARAGE
21-8 x 22-10

cl

(optional full bath)

Direct from the Mediterranean, this European-style one-story home offers a practical floor plan. The facade features arch-top, multi-paned windows, a columned front porch, a tall chimney stack and a tiled roof. The interior offers a wealth of livability. What you'll appreciate first is the juxtaposition of the great room and the formal dining room—both defined by columns. A more casual eating area is attached to the L-shaped kitchen and features access to a screened porch—as does the great room. Three bedrooms mean abundant sleeping space. Two family bedrooms share a full hall bath, while the master suite boasts a private bath on the opposite side of the house. The study could be a fourth bedroom—choose the full bath option in this case. A tray ceiling decorates the master suite. The master bath includes a separate shower and tub, a walk-in closet and double sinks. You can also access the porch from the master bedroom. A two-car garage and a laundry room complete this plan.

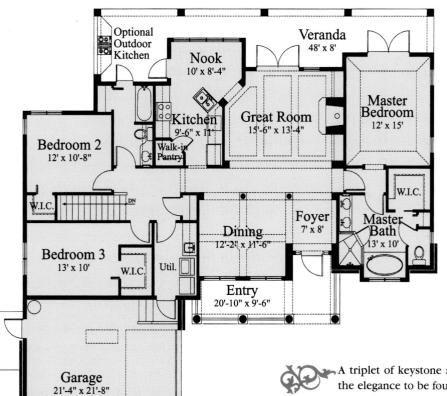

Optional Outdoor Kitchen

Veranda
48' x 8'

Nook
10' x 8'-4"

Kitchen
9'-6" x 11'

Walk-in Pantry

Great Room
15'-6" x 13'-4"

Master Bedroom
12' x 15'

Bedroom 2
12' x 10'-8"

W.I.C.

DN

W.I.C.

Dining
12'-2" x 11'-6"

Foyer
7' x 8'

Master Bath
13' x 10'

Bedroom 3
13' x 10'

W.I.C.

Util.

Entry
20'-10" x 9'-6"

Garage
21'-4" x 21'-8"

DESIGN HPT220026

Square Footage: 1,717
Width: 58'-0"
Depth: 62'-0"

A triplet of keystone arches mimicking recessed fanlight windows hints at the elegance to be found within this charming European-style home. Stucco and stone and classical porch columns highlight the beauty of the exterior. Vast amenities await within this compact one-story design. Inside, columns define the formal dining and great rooms. Both the great room and the master suite boast French doors that open to the expansive veranda with its optional outdoor kitchen—perfect for summer afternoons. An alluring fireplace warms the great room. Space is masterfully used in the master suite with its walk-in closet, double-sink vanity, separate shower, tub and compartmented bath. The left side of the plan holds two family bedrooms that share a full bath, a utility room and the two-car garage. Both of the family bedrooms also provide walk-in closets. Don't miss the sunny nook overlooking the veranda and the well-equipped kitchen with a walk-in pantry.

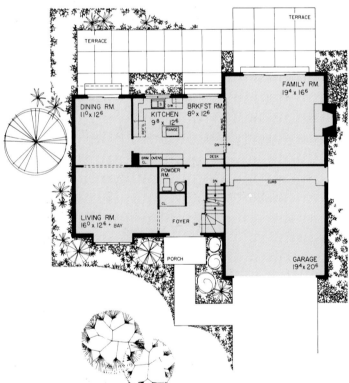

DESIGN HPT220027

First Floor: 1,149 sq. ft.

Second Floor: 850 sq. ft.

Total: 1,999 sq. ft.

Width: 50'-0"

Depth: 38'-8"

LD

With rustic French essence, this petite brick manor offers neighborhood-friendly appeal and a floor plan sure to please—perfectly suited to any countryside setting. Corner quoins, a front bay window and elegant double doors add to the charm and physique of the exterior, while family efficiency reigns within. The living and dining rooms offer a formal setting, while the more casual kitchen/breakfast area and family room extend comfort. The kitchen is a gourmet's delight with an island workstation, plenty of counter space and breathtaking views of the backyard. The dining room, family room, kitchen and breakfast room overlook the rear terrace, which is large enough to host a variety of outdoor events. The master bedroom features a private bath and spacious closet space. Three additional family bedrooms are available and share a full hall bath. One bedroom can easily be converted to a quiet study. A garage downstairs completes the plan.

DESIGN HPT220028

First Floor: 924 sq. ft.
Second Floor: 1,052 sq. ft.
Total: 1,976 sq. ft.
Width: 44'-8"
Depth: 36'-0"

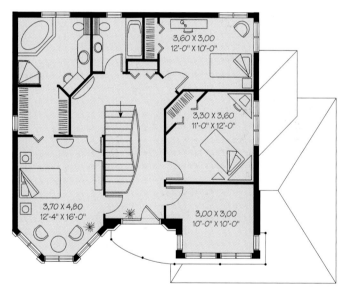

3,60 X 3,00
12'-0" X 10'-0"

3,30 X 3,60
11'-0" X 12'-0"

3,70 X 4,80
12'-4" X 16'-0"

3,00 X 3,00
10'-0" X 10'-0"

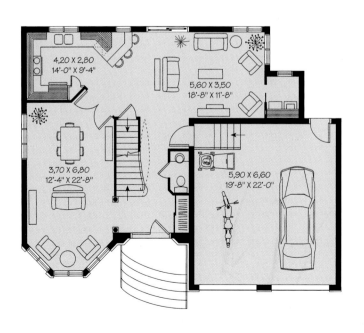

4,20 X 2,80
14'-0" X 9'-4"

5,60 X 3,50
18'-8" X 11'-8"

3,70 X 6,80
12'-4" X 22'-8"

5,90 X 6,60
19'-8" X 22'-0"

This magnificent European adaptation is highlighted by hipped roofs, an abundance of beautiful windows, cornice detailing and an elegant glass entrance door adjacent to an impressive two-story turret. An iron railing dramatically enhances the second-floor porch. Inside, a magnificent living and dining area is illuminated by a bay window. The U-shaped kitchen features a useful breakfast bar and a corner pantry. The comfortable family room is located to the rear of the plan, behind the two-car garage. A gracious staircase leads upstairs to a deluxe master suite, which indulges with a brilliant bay window, enormous whirlpool bath and walk-through closet. Two additional family bedrooms share a full hall bath. The third room on this floor would make a perfect home office, nursery or playroom. Double doors from the hallway open onto a petite veranda, overlooking the entrance and front yard—a perfect plant ledge. This home is designed with a basement foundation.

DESIGN HPT220029

Square Footage: 2,300
Width: 58'-10"
Depth: 83'-0"

mbr
14 x 15-4

porch

brkfst
12-6 X 14-6

m bath

12-10 X 15-4

family
18-6 X 19

kit

br.2
11 X 11

br.3
(opt. study)
11-8 X 11

foyer

dining
11 X 14

laundry

br.4
11 X 12-4

garage
21 X 21

This French Provencal charmer includes a stunning mix of stucco and brick on the exterior, which achieves the flavor of classic European styling. The arched entrance provides a dramatic first impression. Beyond the foyer, the family room is at the heart of the home and provides a fireplace and access to a covered porch at the rear. This area is perfect for entertaining guests. A formal dining room is found to the right of the foyer and easily connects to the kitchen. A breakfast bay serves the island kitchen and overlooks the rear yard. The master suite is tucked away at the rear of the plan with a luxurious bath and walk-in closet. Two family bedrooms—or make one a study—sit just off the family room. One additional bedroom with a full bath, and a utility room reside near the garage entrance.

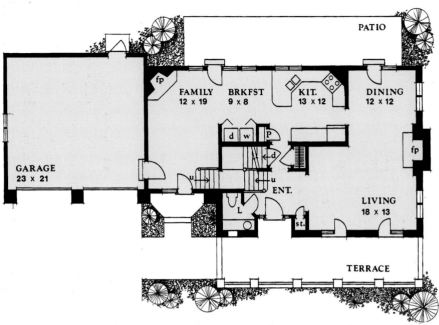

Design HPT220030

First Floor: 1,132 sq. ft.
Second Floor: 968 sq. ft.
Total: 2,100 sq. ft.
Width: 70'-6"
Depth: 37'-1"

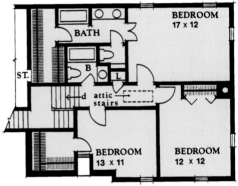

Bricks and stucco, tall shutters and interesting roof details create a picturesque European-style cottage, dazzled in French Country accents. A front terrace and a rear patio provide extra space for entertaining and relaxing, and a massive arched entranceway welcomes you inside with graceful style. To the right of the entry, the formal living and dining rooms center on an imposing fireplace—one of two in the home. The second fireplace is located in the family room, which offers a secondary front door, as well as access to the patio. Casual meals will be enjoyed in the breakfast area, which is convenient to the kitchen. A second access to the patio is found in the dining room. A two-car garage completes the first floor. A master suite, with a private bath and a walk-in closet, and two family bedrooms occupy the second floor. Stairs to the attic can be accessed from the second-floor hallway.

DESIGN HPT220031

First Floor: 1,715 sq. ft.
Second Floor: 620 sq. ft.
Total: 2,335 sq. ft.
Bonus Room: 265 sq. ft.
Width: 58'-6"
Depth: 50'-3"

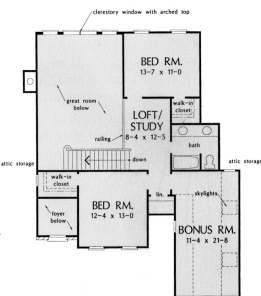

clerestory window with arched top

BED RM.
13-7 x 11-0

great room below

LOFT/ STUDY
8-4 x 12-5

walk-in closet

railing — down

bath

attic storage

walk-in closet

BED RM.
12-4 x 13-0

lin.

skylights

attic storage

foyer below

BONUS RM.
11-4 x 21-8

QUOTE ONE®

Cost to build? See page 182
to order complete cost estimate
to build this house in your area!

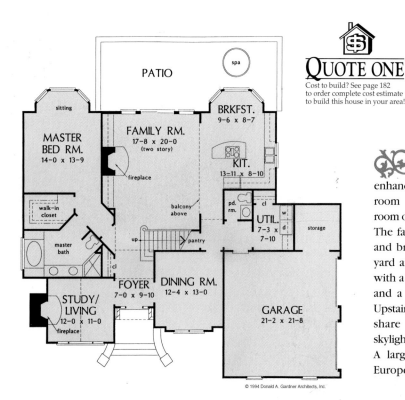

PATIO

spa

sitting

MASTER BED RM.
14-0 x 13-9

FAMILY RM.
17-8 x 20-0
(two story)

BRKFST.
9-6 x 8-7

fireplace

KIT.
13-11 x 8-10

walk-in closet

balcony above

pd. rm.

cl

UTIL.
7-3 x 7-10

w d

storage

master bath

up

pantry

cl

STUDY/ LIVING
12-0 x 11-0

FOYER
7-0 x 9-10

DINING RM.
12-4 x 13-0

GARAGE
21-2 x 21-8

fireplace

© 1994 Donald A. Gardner Architects, Inc.

With a decidedly European flavor, this two-story home offers great livability. Classic stone and stucco formality enhances the exterior appearance. The foyer opens to a study or living room on the left—warmed by an enchanting fireplace. The dining room on the right offers large proportions and full illuminating windows. The family room with fireplace remains open to the island kitchen and breakfast room. Here, a sunny bay window overlooks the rear yard and patio. The rear patio is an entertaining dream—complete with a cozy spa. In the master suite, a bayed sitting area, walk-in closet and a pampering bath with a whirlpool tub make a fine retreat. Upstairs, two bedrooms flank a loft or study area. These family bedrooms share a full hall bath. The bonus room—brightened by beautiful skylights—easily converts to a guest bedroom, home office or playroom. A large two-car garage with extra storage completes this rustic European plan.

CAREFREE CHÂTEAUX

"To accomplish great things, we must not only act, but also dream; not only plan, but also believe."
—Anatole France
French author
Nobel Prize recipient
1844-1924

Photo by Living Concepts Home Planning

Design HPT220032

First Floor: 2,398 sq. ft.
Second Floor: 657 sq. ft.
Total: 3,055 sq. ft.
Bonus Room: 374 sq. ft.
Width: 72'-8"
Depth: 69'-1"

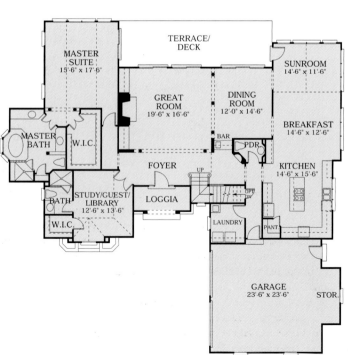

European formality is met with a bold spirit in this splendid transitional French plan. Corner quoins, stone accents and French shutters decorate the exterior of this beautiful stucco home. Perfect for a lake or golf course setting, this home offers walls of windows in the living areas. Soak up the scenery in the sun room, which opens from the breakfast nook and leads to a rear terrace or deck. Ten-foot ceilings preside throughout the first floor, allowing interior vistas and adding volume to the rooms. The library features a tray ceiling and arched window, and would make an excellent home office or guest room suite. Classical columns divide the great room and dining room, which features a see-through wet bar. The deluxe master suite uses defining columns between the bedroom and the lavish bath and walk-in closet. Upstairs, there are two additional suites and a bonus room. Please specify basement or crawlspace foundation when ordering.

Photo by Home Design Services, Inc.

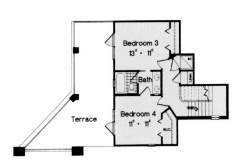

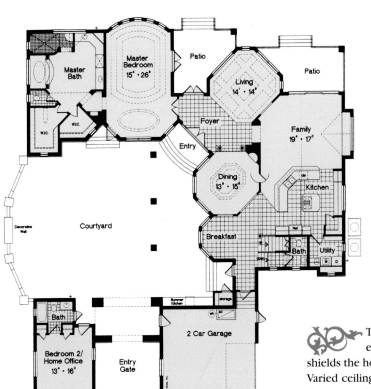

Design HPT220033

First Floor: 2,854 sq. ft.
Second Floor: 484 sq. ft.
Total: 3,338 sq. ft.
Width: 77'-4"
Depth: 94'-0"

This award-winning design showcases French style in a stone-and-stucco exterior. The courtyard, accessed by a charming wrought-iron gate, shields the home from street noise and allows space for private outdoor gatherings. Varied ceiling treatments—a beamed ceiling in the living room and tray ceilings in the master bedroom and dining room—create an exciting interior. Living spaces reside to the right of the plan: the dining room, breakfast area and kitchen cluster around the spacious family room, where sliding glass doors open to a rear patio. The master suite also offers patio access; other luxurious appointments in this suite include two large walk-in closets and a grand bath with an arched entry. A front bedroom with two closets and a private bath can double as a convenient home office; two more bedrooms with access to a terrace reside upstairs.

Design HPT220034

First Floor: 1,735 sq. ft.
Second Floor: 1,355 sq. ft.
Total: 3,090 sq. ft.
Width: 54'-0"
Depth: 71'-0"

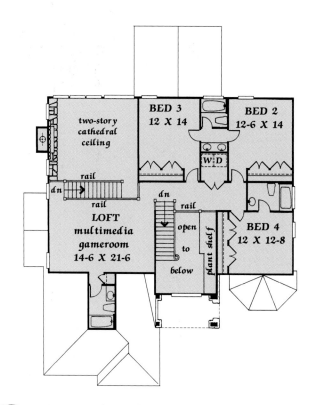

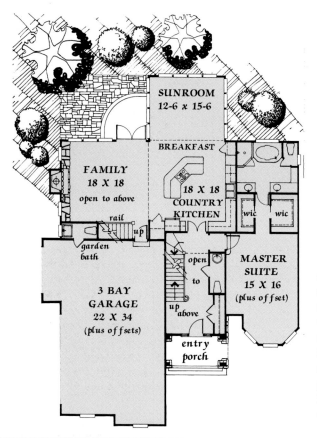

A stucco and stone facade creates a luxurious appearance for this infallible French design. The turret-style bay lends palatial elegance to the dashing sophistication of the overall plan. Upon entry through the magnificently arched doorway, the two-story foyer leads to a lavish country kitchen, which becomes the center of this well-laid-out home. A sun room floods the breakfast nook and kitchen with brilliant natural light. The comfortable family room features an open cathedral ceiling and French doors exiting the rear of the home onto a quaint terrace. A round bay window sheds lots of light into the master suite. Two walk-in closets, a whirlpool tub and dual vanities make the master suite incredibly livable. Upstairs, the loft area is perfect for a multimedia game room and offers a full bath. Bedrooms 2 and 3 share a bath between them. Bedroom 4 provides its own private bath. A two-car garage with a garden bath downstairs completes this design.

Design HPT220035

First Floor: 1,805 sq. ft.
Second Floor: 765 sq. ft.
Total: 2,570 sq. ft.
Bonus Room: 140 sq. ft.
Width: 60'-6"
Depth: 56'-6"

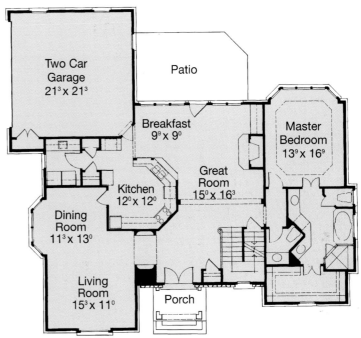

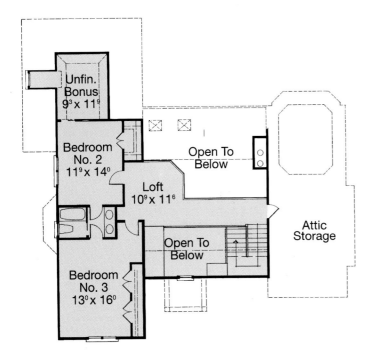

Stone and stucco—with the delicate addition of a latticed front porch—present this French Country home with a gracious welcome. Open living spaces invite casual times in the expansive great room with a full measure of windows and a fireplace rising the full two stories. An adjoining breakfast room with patio doors provides a casual place for meals with easy access from the kitchen. From the gourmet kitchen, the formal dining room is served through a rear passage. Entertaining is a joy here with the added beauty of a bay window in the dining room and a box-bay in the formal living room. The secluded master suite is fashioned with a formal ceiling and a spacious bath highlighted with a spa tub and a walk-in closet. Upstairs, the balcony hall that overlooks the great room leads to a loft and two secondary bedrooms that share a private bath. This home is designed with a walkout basement foundation.

Design HPT220036

First Floor: 2,145 sq. ft.

Second Floor: 1,310 sq. ft.

Total: 3,455 sq. ft.

Bonus Room: 308 sq. ft.

Width: 67'-0"

Depth: 59'-4"

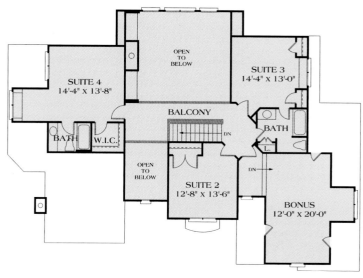

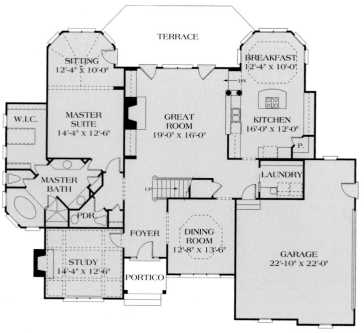

Unusual chimneys, varied rooflines and European window treatments enhance the stone-and-stucco exterior of this breathtaking home. A petite portico welcomes you into the two-story foyer. Inside, the heart of the home is the great room, featuring a fireplace flanked by bookcases, a snack bar and two doors to the rear terrace. A semi-circle of windows outlines the breakfast nook, which opens off the kitchen, a wonderful work area with a cooktop island, a walk-in pantry and ample counter space. The formal dining room is a few steps from both the kitchen and the front door, making entertaining easy. To the left of the foyer, a study with a beam ceiling and a second fireplace serves as a quiet retreat. The first-floor master suite is sure to please with a sunny sitting area, a large walk-in closet and a pampering bath. A second-floor balcony connects three family bedrooms, two baths and a bonus room.

DESIGN HPT220037

First Floor: 1,686 sq. ft.

Second Floor: 1,379 sq. ft.

Total: 3,065 sq. ft.

Width: 72'-0"

Depth: 60'-0"

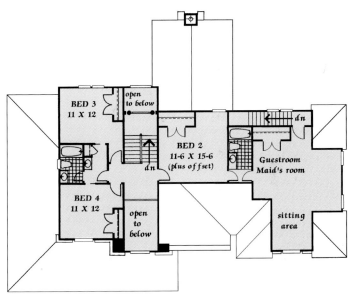

BED 3
11 X 12

open
to below

BED 2
11-6 X 15-6
(plus offset)

dn

Guestroom
Maid's room

BED 4
11 X 12

open
to
below

dn

sitting
area

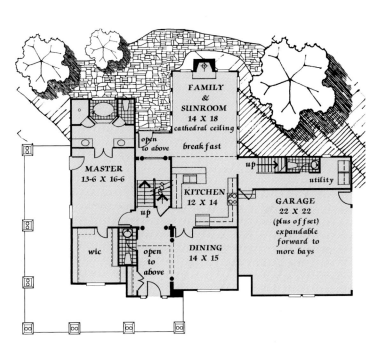

FAMILY
&
SUNROOM
14 X 18
cathedral ceiling

open
to above

breakfast

up

utility

MASTER
13-6 X 16-6

KITCHEN
12 X 14

up

GARAGE
22 X 22
(plus offset)
expandable
forward to
more bays

wic

open to
above

DINING
14 X 15

Segmental dormers, gables and a hipped roof provide interest to this French Country charmer with a wraparound porch. Long arches and a beautiful brick facade dazzle the exterior. Rounded columns adorn the dining room set near the entry. The master suite features a large walk-in closet and a sumptuous bath entered through double doors, which includes a tub overlooking the terrace, a separate shower and double vanities. The kitchen sits at the center of the main floor and features a serving bar to the hearth-warmed family and sun rooms, enhanced by a cathedral ceiling. This area also overlooks the rear terrace—perfect for outdoor entertainment or a simple family patio picnic. A garage, powder room and utility room complete the first floor. Three family bedrooms reside on the second floor near a guest or maid's suite with a bright sitting area—this room sits above the garage. The family bedrooms share a full hall bath.

DESIGN HPT220038

Square Footage: 2,425
Width: 65'-4"
Depth: 52'-2"

This European-style dream home is a family-friendly design. A brick veneer, enormous arched windows and stately brick columns impress on the exterior. Inside, beyond the welcoming porch, the foyer is flanked on either side by formal living and dining rooms. The living room can double as a sophisticated study—perfect for quiet evenings at home. Straight ahead, the great room boasts a wealth of amenities, including a warming fireplace, media center, built-ins and access to the rear covered grilling porch—great for barbecue afternoons. The kitchen, which conveniently resides between the formal dining room and casual breakfast room, offers a high bar and a large pantry. To the right of the plan, the master suite provides private access to the porch, a luxury walk-in closet and a lavish master bath with a whirlpool tub. On the opposite side of the home, three family bedrooms share a full hall bath. Two of the bedrooms boast walk-in closets, and one bedroom will make a perfect home office. A two-car garage and a laundry room complete this plan. Please specify basement, crawlspace or slab foundation when ordering.

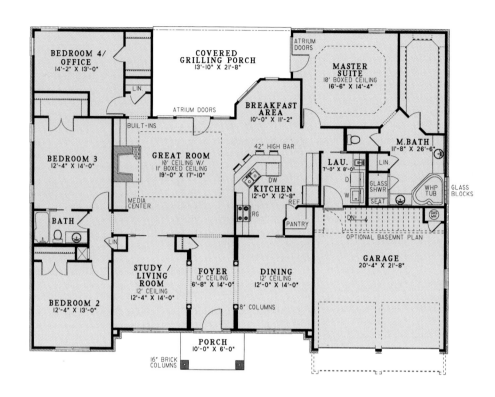

DESIGN HPT220039

First Floor: 1,597 sq. ft.
Second Floor: 1,859 sq. ft.
Total: 3,456 sq. ft.
Width: 62'-0"
Depth: 46'-0"

Corner quoins, keystone lintels and a Palladian window denote European influence in this charming, brick, four-bedroom home. A lovely arch over the entranceway and front porch makes a graceful first impression. The welcoming foyer is flanked on either side by the formal living and dining rooms. A beautiful built-in media center and shelving system surrounds the fireplace in the great room straight ahead. French doors in the great room access the grilling porch, extending the livable space outdoors. The kitchen boasts plenty of counter space as it overlooks the casual breakfast room. A petite powder room is located on the opposite side of the stairs. A bay window lights the master bedroom, and the sumptuous bath with its whirlpool tub adds elegance. An enormous three-car garage completes the first floor, along with a useful laundry room. Three secondary bedrooms featuring walk-in closets are located upstairs and share a full bath. Please specify basement or crawlspace foundation when ordering.

Design HPT220040

First Floor: 1,592 sq. ft.

Second Floor: 1,259 sq. ft.

Total: 2,851 sq. ft.

Width: 56'-0"

Depth: 53'-6"

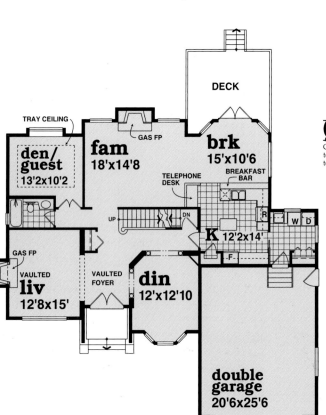

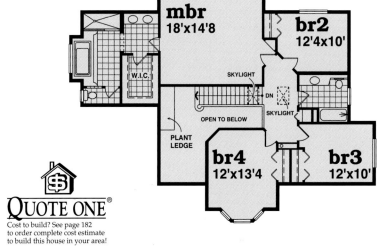

Quote One®

Cost to build? See page 182
to order complete cost estimate
to build this house in your area!

A combination of European architectural details makes this home elegant: keystone arches, shuttered windows, a two-story bay with a copper roof, and a recessed entry. Stucco and stone dazzle the radiant exterior. Inside, a vaulted foyer makes a grand first impression. A formal living room with a fireplace and a dining room with a beautiful bay window flank the foyer on either side. The hearth-warmed family room sits to the rear of the plan, near the island kitchen and breakfast bay. Double doors lead from the bay to an outdoor deck. A den—or guest room—with a tray ceiling offers the use of a full hall bath. Look for the master suite on the second floor, just off a skylit hall. It features a walk-in closet and private bath with separate tub and shower. The other three bedrooms share the use of a full hall bath. A full basement could be finished later for additional space.

DESIGN HPT220041

First Floor: 1,536 sq. ft.
Second Floor: 1,183 sq. ft.
Total: 2,719 sq. ft.
Width: 56'-0"
Depth: 48'-0"

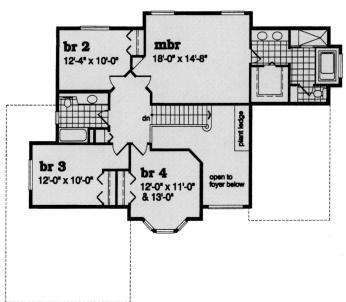

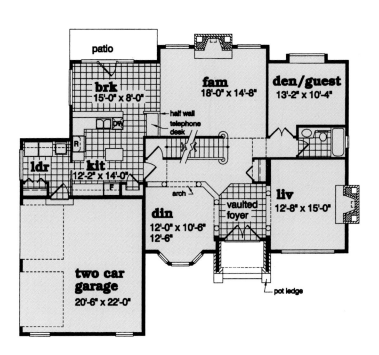

European-style details add distinctive touches to this design: stucco with stonework, a volume roof and a beautiful two-story bay. Stately stone columns make a dramatic first impression, as they frame a double-door entrance into the home. The vaulted foyer is flanked by formal spaces defined by arches: a living room with a fireplace and a dining room with a brilliant bay window. The hearth-warmed family room lies to the rear, near the island kitchen and breakfast room that opens onto a patio. A den or guest room is tucked into the right corner of the plan, near a full bath. The useful laundry room is placed near the kitchen. Upstairs, the bedrooms include a master suite and three family bedrooms. Note the lavish master bath with its walk-in closet, dual sinks, compartmented lavatory and separate tub and shower. A two-car garage is reached through a service entry near the laundry alcove.

Design HPT220042

First Floor: 2,298 sq. ft.
Second Floor: 1,056 sq. ft.
Total: 3,354 sq. ft.
Width: 62'-8"
Depth: 62'-0"

SUITE 2
12'-0" x 14'-0"

BATH

SUITE 3
12'-0" x 14'-0"

W.I.C.

ATTIC

BALCONY

W.I.C.

BATH

W.I.C.

DN

SUITE 4
14'-8" x 13'-10"

OPEN
TO
BELOW

SCREENED
PORCH

BREAKFAST
10'-4" x 8'-0"

DECK

MASTER
SUITE
15'-0" x 18'-6"

FAMILY
ROOM
17'-6" x 18'-6"

KITCHEN
12'-0" x 14'-4"

LIVING
ROOM
16'-0" x 14'-0"

W.I.C.

W.I.C.

P. PDR.

OPT
ON

UP

LAUN.

DINING
ROOM
14'-4" x 13'-10"

MASTER
BATH

FOYER

PORTICO

A high hipped roof, intricate brickwork and a copper accent at the front entry highlight the exterior of this European-style design. An interesting chimney is supported by a fireplace in the family room, which combines with the kitchen and breakfast room to create a large informal area on the first floor. Built-in bookcases flanking the fireplace, an island cooktop and plenty of windows are special features in this area. Outdoor living is enhanced by a screened porch and a deck—the latter with access from the breakfast room, living room and master bedroom. Formal areas include a dining room to the left of the foyer, and the living room. The master suite fills the right side of the plan and boasts twin walk-in closets and vanities. The second floor offers three bedrooms— one with a private bath—and an attic for storage. The full basement houses a garage and space for a recreation area.

Design HPT220043

First Floor: 2,050 sq. ft.
Second Floor: 561 sq. ft.
Total: 2,611 sq. ft.
Bonus Room: 272 sq. ft.
Width: 64'-10"
Depth: 64'-0"

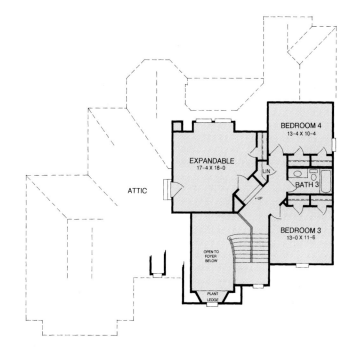

Old World ambiance characterizes this European-style home, which boasts a gentle French influence, along with Tudor details. The elegant stone entrance opens to the two-story foyer. A well-proportioned dining room is viewed through an arch flanked by columns. The oversized octagonal great room features a coffered ceiling and a see-through fireplace that can also be seen from the kitchen and breakfast rooms. While the kitchen offers a pantry, the bayed breakfast area shares access to the rear porch with the master suite across the way. The master suite includes a luxury bath, walk-in closet and a cozy sitting area off the bedroom. A second bedroom on the first floor acts as a nursery, guest room or study. A two-car garage with storage and a utility room completes this floor. Upstairs, two spacious bedrooms share a bath. An expandable area is available for future use. Please specify basement, crawlspace or slab foundation when ordering.

DESIGN HPT220044

Square Footage: 2,504
Width: 65'-0"
Depth: 59'-10"

A brick exterior, cast-stone trim and corner quoins make up this attractive single-living-area design. The lovely arched windows are distinctly European, along with the hipped-roof silhouette. Inside, the front porch gives way to an elegant entry, which extends to a gallery hall. The formal dining room resides across from the living room, which offers a fireplace and built-in entertainment center. The large living area opens to the kitchen/breakfast room, all with ten-foot ceilings. A large bay window enhances the breakfast room with a full glass door to the covered rear patio. A large master suite with vaulted ceilings features a luxurious master bath with double lavatories and an oversized walk-in closet. Bedroom 2 also offers its own private bath with a shower and a walk-in closet. Bedrooms 3 and 4 reside on the opposite side of the home and share a full bath between them. A utility room, which opens to the three-car garage, completes this home plan.

DESIGN HPT220045

First Floor: 1,750 sq. ft.
Second Floor: 855 sq. ft.
Total: 2,605 sq. ft.
Width: 77'-0"
Depth: 58'-0"

Second Floor

BEDROOM 15' x 12'
BATH
DRESS.
BEDROOM 15' x 13'
HALL
TO ATTIC
HEAT & A.C.
DN
OPEN TO LOWER LEVEL
BALCONY
BEDROOM 13' x 12'
PORCH 34' x 6'
RAILING

First Floor

GARAGE 22' x 22'
EATING 10' x 10'
STORAGE 10' x 8'
UTIL.
HIS
PORCH
LINEN
BATH
LINEN
LIVING 20' x 19'
KITCHEN 14' x 13'
ISLAND
MASTER SUITE 20' x 12'
HERS
BOOKS
WH STOR.
HEAT & A.C.
FOYER (OPEN TO UPPER LEVEL)
UP
DINING 13' x 12'
SITTING
PORCH 34' x 6'

Nine-foot ceilings and shaded upper and lower porticos make this a perfect retreat for long, hot summers. French styling—romantic for a country or riverside setting—sets a luxurious tone. An arched glass entrance welcomes you inside to the two-story foyer. The living room is cozy any time of the year with built-ins, a fireplace and a raised tray ceiling. The island countertop kitchen is conveniently set between the formal dining room and the casual eating area. The first-floor master suite offers its own porch retreat, a pampering bath with His and Hers vanities, walk-in closets, compartmented toilet and separate tub and shower. Upstairs, a balcony hallway overlooks the foyer. Three family bedrooms share a full bath on the second floor. One bedroom privately accesses the second-floor porch. A storage room in the garage prevents climbing up to the hot attic. Please specify basement, crawlspace or slab foundation when ordering.

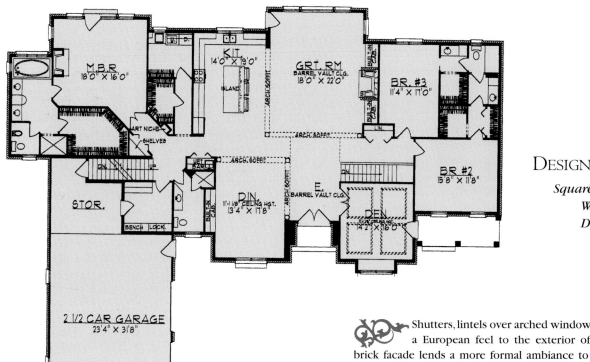

DESIGN HPT220046

Square Footage: 3,386
Width: 95'-0"
Depth: 73'-8"

Shutters, lintels over arched windows, and a hipped roofline lend a European feel to the exterior of this ranch-style home. The brick facade lends a more formal ambiance to the overall plan. Inside, the floor plan is thoughtfully laid out and is perfect for any growing family. The foyer offers a unique vaulted barrel ceiling and opens to the dining room, den and great room. The amenity-filled den features an eleven-foot ceiling, a window seat and a door that opens to a side porch. Arched soffits and columns lend elegance to the dining room and great room. The great room also includes a vaulted barrel ceiling, fireplace and built-in cabinets. The master suite is adorned with art niches, double doors, a fireplace, an immense walk-in closet and an elegant private bath. Two additional bedrooms reside at the other end of the house—they share a bath and enjoy walk-in closets. A useful two-car garage completes this family plan.

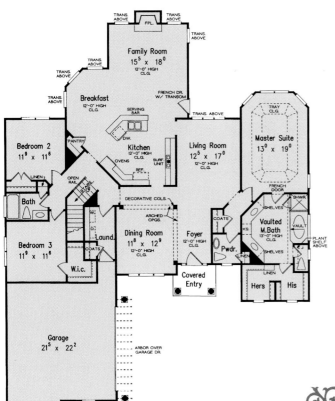

DESIGN HPT220047

Square Footage: 2,282
Bonus Space: 629 sq. ft.
Width: 60'-0"
Depth: 75'-4"

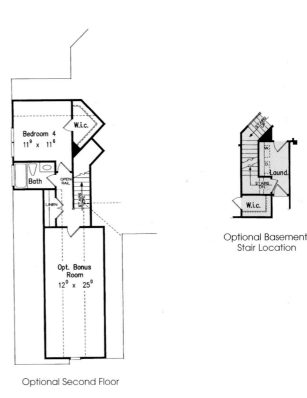

Optional Second Floor

Optional Basement Stair Location

Columns and keystone lintels lend a European aura to this stone-and-siding home, which combines cottage simplicity with Chateau styling. Arched openings and decorative columns define the formal dining room to the left of the foyer. A ribbon of windows with transoms above draws sunshine into the living room. The master suite opens from a short hallway, and enjoys a tray ceiling illuminated by a bay window, a vaulted master bath with shelving, a compartmented toilet, garden tub and His and Hers walk-in closets. Transoms abound in the open informal living areas of this home. A bayed breakfast nook adjoins the kitchen with a central serving bar and the family room with a warming fireplace. A useful pantry is available to the left of the kitchen. Two additional bedrooms share a full bath to the left of the plan. Bedroom 3 offers a huge walk-in closet. A laundry room, connected to the two-car garage completes this floor plan. Please specify basement or crawlspace foundation when ordering.

DESIGN HPT220048

First Floor: 2,174 sq. ft.
Second Floor: 877 sq. ft.
Total: 3,051 sq. ft.
Width: 76'-0"
Depth: 56'-0"

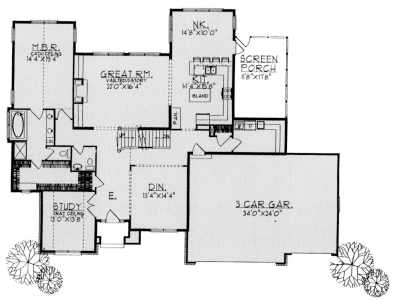

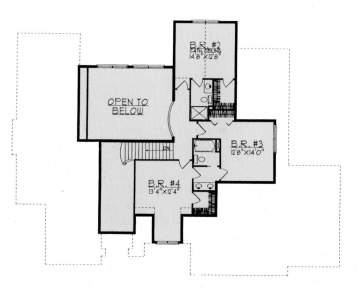

This two-story French manor home welcomes you—the amount of space in this home will give you plenty of room to grow. Imagine the possibilities of four bedrooms, three stalls in the garage and 3,051 square feet! From the entry, the French doors open into a study with a tray ceiling. On the other side of the entry, you will appreciate the formal dining room. Straight through the entry, a vaulted two-story ceiling, a fireplace, built-in shelves and stunning windows that overlook the backyard will amaze you. From the great room, enter the kitchen where you will appreciate the size and efficiency, along with the pantry, island and snack bar. From the kitchen, imagine how you'll love the breakfast nook, which overlooks the backyard and the screened porch. Also located on the main floor is a spectacular master bedroom. You will fall in love with the cathedral ceiling, the considerable master bath and the spacious walk-in closet with a built-in bench.

DESIGN HPT220049

First Floor: 2,508 sq. ft.
Second Floor: 960 sq. ft.
Total: 3,468 sq. ft.
Width: 79'-8"
Depth: 70'-0"

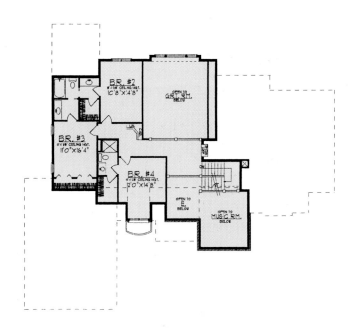

At first sight, the charm of this home will invite you inside. You will adore the traditional French style of this two-story, three-car garage, 3,468 square-foot home. You can't help but love the balcony that stretches from a second floor bedroom. You are sure to appreciate the uniqueness of a music room with a generous arched window. You will also be pleased with the French doors that welcome you to a study that overlooks the backyard. Certainly, you will be enticed by the arched soffit that invites you into the great room. An astonishing fireplace, built-in cabinets and an enormous arched window overlooks the backyard from the great room. The kitchen provides great use of space with a built-in desk, island workstation and walk-in pantry. The screened porch is accessible from the nook and the deck. The master bedroom leaves nothing to be desired and includes built-in cabinets with French doors that open to the master bathroom.

Design HPT220050

First Floor: 2,502 sq. ft.
Second Floor: 677 sq. ft.
Total: 3,179 sq. ft.
Bonus Room: 171 sq. ft.
Width: 71'-2"
Depth: 56'-10"

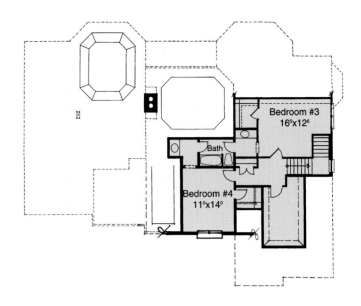

Stucco and stone and mesmerizing Mediterranean style add to the plush atmosphere created by this radiant design. This dynamic elevation features wing walls and an elegant window-framed doorway. The foyer is flanked on either side by the quiet study and the formal dining room. Straight ahead, the great room offers a wall of windows and an enormous fireplace. The kitchen overlooks the bayed breakfast and sun rooms. The rear deck can be accessed from either the sun room or the master suite. The master suite is a pampering haven with an indulging bath and a spacious walk-in closet. Bedroom 2, which features its own private bath and walk-in closet, will make an ideal guest suite. The second floor is accessed by a private staircase located between the garage and kitchen. Bedrooms 3 and 4 share a full bath, along with an extra room that could make a fourth bedroom or home office. This home is designed with a walkout basement foundation.

Design HPT220051

First Floor: 1,383 sq. ft.
Second Floor: 1,576 sq. ft.
Total: 2,959 sq. ft.
Width: 65'-0"
Depth: 46'-0"

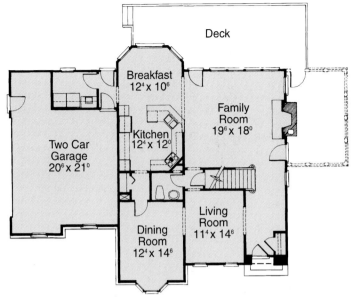

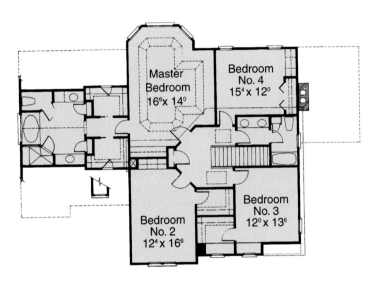

Stucco, stone and a cozy side arbor set a cheerful tone for this French design. Inside, the formal living room or parlor leads to a formal dining room with an elegant bay window. A butler's pantry serves the counter-abundant kitchen and the bayed breakfast nook. The family room includes a warming fireplace and access to both the arbor and the rear deck. The rear deck is perfect for outdoor activities, especially in the summer and the arbor is a romantic hideaway for quiet evenings. A two-car garage and laundry room complete the first floor. Upstairs, three family bedrooms share a full bath and plenty of closet space. The master suite features a bay window, a large sitting area, dual walk-in closets and vanities, a compartmented toilet and a separate shower and tub. This home is designed with a walkout basement foundation.

Design HPT220052

Square Footage: 2,451
Width: 59'-3"
Depth: 85'-9"

garage
19-4 X 20

covered
walkway

mbr
16-10 X 13

m bath

brkfst
12-2 X 10

kit
13-2 X 12-8

family
18 X 30-11

br.2
12 X 11

laundry

dining
12-10 X 11

foyer

br.4
11-6 X 12

br.3
12 X 13-1

Decorative finials atop the steeply pitched, wood-shingle roof and arched dormers make this French Eclectic home distinctive. A stucco and brick exterior makes a formal first impression. A separate garage toward the rear is practical. The home is reached from the rear by a covered walkway that leads to the breakfast and kitchen area, and a set of double doors that open into the family room. The gourmet kitchen offers plenty of counter space and an island workstation. The family room with a fireplace is the heart of the home and all rooms seem to radiate around this central gathering area. There are four bedrooms in all, including the pampering master suite with its walk-in closet and large, elegant bathroom. The bath features a corner tub brightened by a window, a separate shower, two vanities and a compartmented toilet. Three other bedrooms share a bathroom centrally located to all. A formal dining room with a guest powder room nearby completes the floor plan.

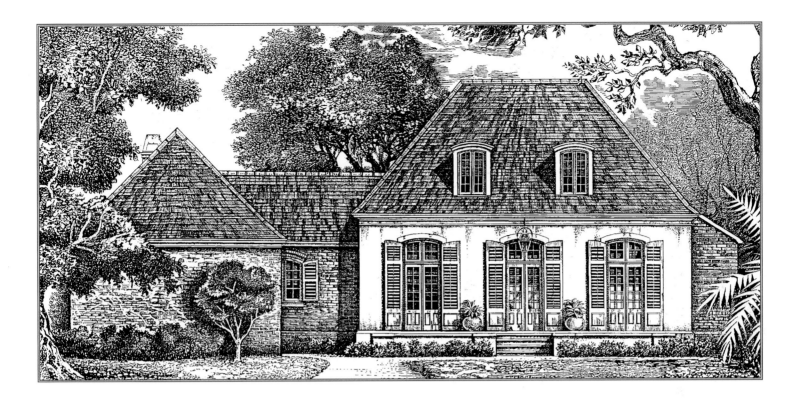

Design HPT220053

First Floor: 2,298 sq. ft.

Second Floor: 731 sq. ft.

Total: 3,029 sq. ft.

Width: 71'-10"

Depth: 78'-0"

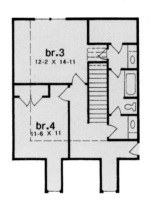

br.3
12-2 X 14-11

br.4
11-6 X 11

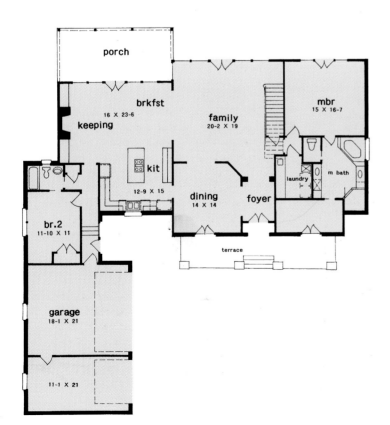

porch

brkfst
16 X 23-6

keeping

family
20-2 X 19

mbr
15 X 16-7

kit
12-9 X 15

laundry

m bath

dining
14 X 14

foyer

br.2
11-10 X 11

terrace

garage
18-1 X 21

11-1 X 21

Beautiful exterior detailing sets this home apart. A hipped roof, quaint dormers, French shutters, slightly arched windows and a stucco finish keep this home in European check. Three sets of French doors open inside from the front terrace. The formal dining room is set to the left of the foyer. The family room, overlooked by a staircase to the second floor, accesses the rear through a set of double doors. The keeping room's fireplace warms both the breakfast room, which accesses a rear porch, and the nearby island kitchen. The laundry room is conveniently located next to the master bedroom suite, which includes a private bath and walk-in closet. A second bedroom with a private bath is located on the opposite side of the home. Upstairs, two bedrooms share a bath that offers separate dressing areas. The family cars can room together, while the Ferrari enjoys a separate bay in the three-car garage.

A mini-estate with French country details, this home preserves the beauty of historical design without sacrificing modern convenience. A hipped silhouette, an arching doorway and stucco styling combine to offer you a taste of charming Europe. An inviting front terrace makes a beautiful first impression. Through double doors, the floor plan opens from a central foyer flanked by a dining room and a study. The family room offers windows overlooking the rear yard and a fireplace. The master bedroom suite features a sitting room that opens to the rear and a bath fit for royalty with walk-in closets. A smaller family bedroom that would make a perfect nursery has a full bath nearby with a walk-in closet. A fireplace in the keeping room warms the breakfast room, which accesses the rear porch that leads to the three-car garage. The island kitchen provides a pantry and a petite office nearby. A third bedroom also enjoys a full bath. A laundry room is tucked away close by.

DESIGN HPT220054

Square Footage: 3,230
Width: 94'-8"
Depth: 88'-5"

Design HPT220055

Square Footage: 2,678
Width: 69'-4"
Depth: 84'-8"

In true French Country style, this home begins with a fenced terrace that protects the double-door entry. A mysterious ambiance surrounds this exquisite Old World design, which is outlined in a stucco and brick exterior finish. The graceful arch of the entrance mimics timeless style, while the quaint window details offer refined elegance. The main foyer separates formal living and dining areas and leads back to a large family room with a fireplace and built-ins. The breakfast room overlooks a wrapping outdoor porch and opens to the island kitchen. Three bedrooms are found on the left side of the plan—two family bedrooms sharing a full bath and a master suite with a sitting area. The private and deluxe master bath, along with a huge walk-in closet, adds pampering amenities to this indulging suite. A fourth bedroom is tucked behind the two-car garage and features a private bath and walk-in closet.

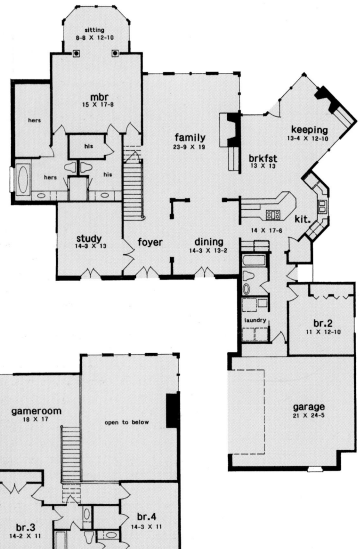

Design HPT220056

First Floor: 2,780 sq. ft.
Second Floor: 878 sq. ft.
Total: 3,658 sq. ft.
Width: 68'-3"
Depth: 89'-1"

The symmetrical front of this home conceals an imaginatively asymmetrical floor plan beyond. The exterior, exquisitely designed with stucco, French shutters and topped with a hipped roof, captures a romantic Old World innocence. A keeping room, a sitting area in the master bedroom and a second bedroom all jut out from this home, forming interesting angles and providing extra window space. Two fireplaces, a game room, a study and His and Hers bathrooms in the master suite are interesting elements in this home. Bedrooms 3 and 4 upstairs share a full bath between them. Bedroom 4 offers its own walk-in closet. The bayed kitchen, with a walk-in pantry and a center island with room for seating, is sure to lure guests and family alike. The open floor plan and two-story ceilings in the family room add a contemporary touch. A two-car garage and a laundry complete this charming plan.

Design HPT220057

First Floor: 2,345 sq. ft.
Second Floor: 663 sq. ft.
Total: 3,008 sq. ft.
Bonus Room: 194 sq. ft.
Width: 62'-10"
Depth: 80'-11"

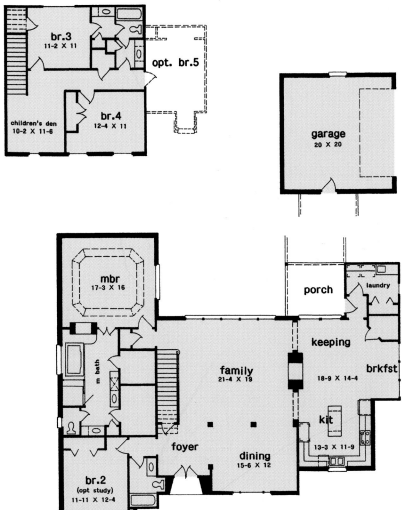

A steeply pitched French-style roof and an Italian-inspired, arched double-door entry create an exterior with international interest. Stucco and brick gracefully drape the exterior. Inside is a thoroughly modern floor plan designed for active families. Upstairs, two family bedrooms share a bathroom. Each has a private vanity area. The children's den is an ideal place to play or study. An additional bedroom upstairs is a space-expanding option in this home for the growing family. Downstairs, the island kitchen opens to the breakfast nook and keeping room. The laundry room is tucked away next to a petite rear porch. From here, a walkway leads to the detached garage. A wall of windows illuminates the family room, warmed by a fireplace. The master suite offers a private and romantic fireplace, as well as a private bath and two huge walk-in closets. An additional bedroom on this floor, next to a full bath, makes a great guest suite, quiet study or nursery.

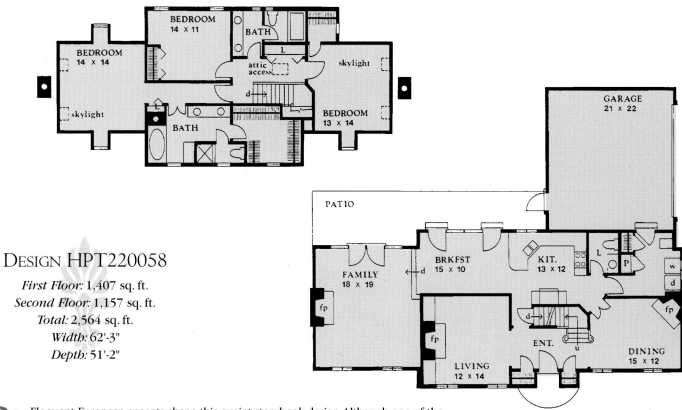

DESIGN HPT220058

First Floor: 1,407 sq. ft.
Second Floor: 1,157 sq. ft.
Total: 2,564 sq. ft.
Width: 62'-3"
Depth: 51'-2"

Eloquent European accents shape this quaint storybook design. Although one of the massive chimneys on this French stucco home is decorative, fireplaces in the family, living and dining rooms will ensure that you have no trouble keeping warm. The front of the house appears symmetrical, but the front door is off-center, adding a bit of eccentricity. The entrance opens into the formal rooms, then leads back to the kitchen, which opens into a breakfast area with French doors to the patio. The sunken family room also accesses the patio. A garage and laundry room complete the first floor. Upstairs, skylights brighten the interior of two of the three bedrooms. The larger bedroom offers its own whirlpool bath, which opens through double doors and extends into a huge walk-in closet. The other two bedrooms share a full hall bath that includes double vanities and a linen closet. An attic can be accessed from the hallway.

DESIGN HPT220059

First Floor: 2,320 sq. ft.
Second Floor: 601 sq. ft.
Total: 2,921 sq. ft.
Width: 59'-0"
Depth: 98'-6"

Stucco styling and French detailing enclose this mystical design. This chateau is packed with luxurious amenities, starting with an open foyer and a wide living space that opens to a private loggia. Walls of rear windows look out to this sumptuous area, which includes a fountain courtyard. The family room is warmed by an enchanting fireplace. A gourmet kitchen with a cooktop island counter serves the formal two-story dining room and breakfast area for more casual occasions. The plan offers three optional sets of doors to the flex room and an office/study, which could easily convert to a guest room. A bathroom across the hall offers privacy to guests. A sequestered master suite offers a garden tub in the master bath and generous wardrobe space. A laundry room and garage with storage complete the first floor. Upstairs, Bedrooms 2 and 3 each offer private full baths and closet space. Each of these bedrooms also provides access to a second-floor porch.

Design HPT220060

Square Footage: 2,526
Width: 64'-0"
Depth: 81'-7"

Interesting angles and creative detailing characterize the exterior of this brick manor. Distinctly European styling and French accents sweep the facade and invite timeless elegance. A lavishly arched entranceway gracefully welcomes all inside to a petite foyer. Inside, the formal dining room is just off the foyer for ease in entertaining. Straight ahead, the formal living room is reserved for more elegant occasions. A gallery hall leads to the island kitchen, which opens to an informal dining area with access to two covered patios. At the rear, a cozy family room is warmed by a quaint fireplace—perfect for casual family gatherings. Sleeping quarters include two family bedrooms that share a bath to the right of the plan and another bedroom, which could be used as a study, on the left. A full hall bath is available to this extra room. The left wing is dedicated to a lavish master suite complete with a vaulted ceiling and sumptuous bath with a whirlpool tub and separate shower. The master suite has private access to the rear patio. A spacious three-car garage completes this plan.

Design HPT220061

First Floor: 2,518 sq. ft.
Second Floor: 1,013 sq. ft.
Total: 3,531 sq. ft.
Bonus Room: 192 sq. ft.
Width: 67'-8"
Depth: 74'-2"

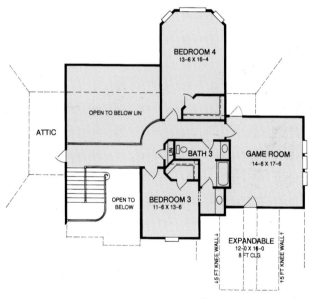

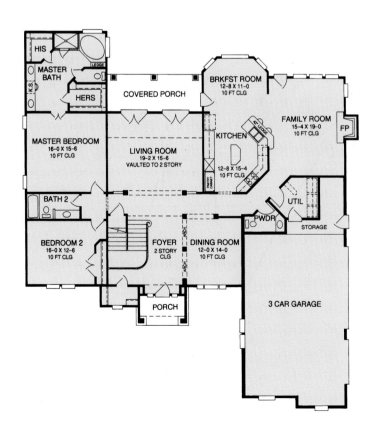

Old World charm gives this design its universal appeal. Brick and stone and arching accents lend a French flavor to the overall plan. Inside, an up-to-date floor plan offers it all. The two-story foyer makes a grand first impression. Two living areas provide space for both formal and informal entertaining. Straight ahead, beyond the foyer, the great room is vaulted to the second floor and opens through two sets of doors to the rear covered porch. The island kitchen and breakfast room overlook the large family room with a cozy fireplace. The master suite, with a lavish bath and His and Hers walk-in closets, is located on the first floor. A secondary bedroom nearby would make a perfect guest suite, study or nursery. An enormous three-car garage with extra storage space completes the first floor. Upstairs, Bedrooms 3 and 4 share a large bath and offer their own walk-in closets. The game room is a perfect entertainment center for the kids or make it a billiard room for the adults. Please specify basement, crawlspace or slab foundation when ordering.

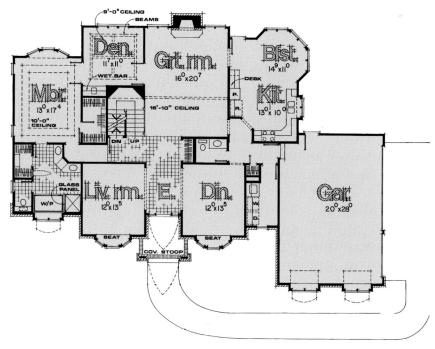

DESIGN HPT220062

First Floor: 2,007 sq. ft.
Second Floor: 838 sq. ft.
Total: 2,845 sq. ft.
Width: 72'-0"
Depth: 48'-8"

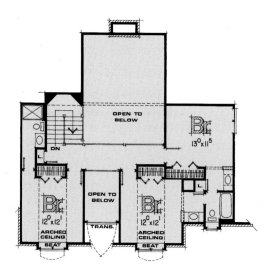

The estate entry on this beautiful European-style home leaves a lasting first impression. Elegant arches and a brick facade topped by a hipped roof extend a sense of formality. Inside is a dynamic floor plan to match its exterior radiance. Formal living areas—the living and dining rooms—flank the tiled entry. Each of these rooms is graced with a window seat. There's also the spacious great room with a fireplace and the beamed-ceiling den with a wet bar for less-formal occasions. The kitchen features an L-shaped work area and a bayed breakfast area for casual family dining. Also downstairs, a large private master suite boasts a bay window and a ten-foot tray ceiling. The lavish master bath is a pampering haven. A three-car garage and laundry facilities complete the first floor. Upstairs are three more bedrooms—two with arched ceilings—two baths and a balcony overlooking the great room. Closet space is abundant.

Design HPT220063

First Floor: 2,504 sq. ft.
Second Floor: 1,000 sq. ft.
Total: 3,504 sq. ft.
Width: 75'-4"
Depth: 67'-0"

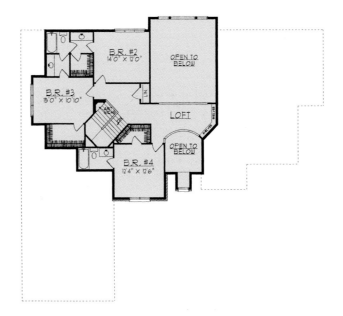

You are sure to love the courtyard entrance to this elegant two-story French home. This 3,500-square-foot home provides you with four bedrooms and a three-car garage. The great room enjoys a view of the backyard, a two-story ceiling and a see-through fireplace to the breakfast nook. The elegant columns in the dining room make the atmosphere perfect for entertaining dinner guests. Perks to be found in the kitchen include an island workstation, a built-in desk, and a walk-in pantry. French doors lead to the master suite on the first floor. You'll love the massive walk-in closet and the master bath, which provides you with all the luxuries that a comfortable home should include. The den will capture you with its grand window and French doors. Impressive features of the second floor include a loft with built-in shelves that overlooks the great room and entry, an art niche along the stairway, a split bedroom and walk-in closets.

Design HPT220064

First Floor: 2,009 sq. ft.
Second Floor: 913 sq. ft.
Total: 2,922 sq. ft.
Bonus Room: 192 sq. ft.
Width: 86'-10"
Depth: 65'-6"

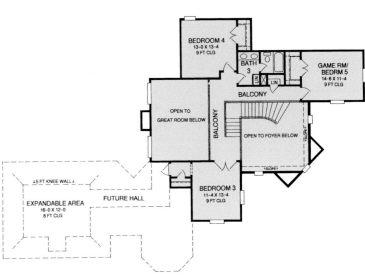

Designed for a pie-shaped or corner lot, this European-style home is a stunner from every angle. Chateau style with French and Tudor accents creates a dramatic appeal. The two-story foyer opens to the huge two-story great room beyond. The kitchen features an angled sink with a window above for views to the rear yard. A large gourmet island has room for a cooktop and plenty of work space. The breakfast room is a sunny bay. The master suite opens to a covered rear porch and includes a luxury bath with His and Hers closets, a corner whirlpool tub and separate shower. A second bedroom and bath is conveniently located on the first floor and can be used as a guest suite, nursery or home office/study. Upstairs, two additional bedrooms share a bath. An additional room can serve as a fifth bedroom or a game room. Expandable area is available over the two-car garage. Please specify basement, crawlspace or slab foundation when ordering.

Design HPT220065

First Floor: 1,980 sq. ft.
Second Floor: 1,317 sq. ft.
Total: 3,297 sq. ft.
Width: 58'-9"
Depth: 66'-9"

Centuries ago, the center column played a vital role in the support of a double-arched window such as the one that graces this home's exterior. Today's amenities combined with the well-seasoned architecture of Europe offer the best of both worlds. A breathtaking blend of stucco and stone encloses a family efficient plan. The contemporary floor plan begins with a soaring foyer that opens to the formal living and dining rooms. The living room enjoys a fireplace, while the nearby open dining room conveniently connects to the kitchen. Casual living is enjoyed at the rear of the plan in the L-shaped island kitchen, the family room with a second fireplace and the light-filled breakfast/sun room. A guest bedroom is tucked behind the family room for privacy and offers its own private bath. Upstairs, an exquisite master suite features a lavish bath and a huge walk-in closet. Two family bedrooms, a full bath and unfinished bonus space complete the second floor. This home is designed with a walkout basement foundation.

Design HPT220066

First Floor: 2,357 sq. ft.
Second Floor: 1,021 sq. ft.
Total: 3,378 sq. ft.
Bonus Room: 168 sq. ft.
Width: 70'-0"
Depth: 62'-6"

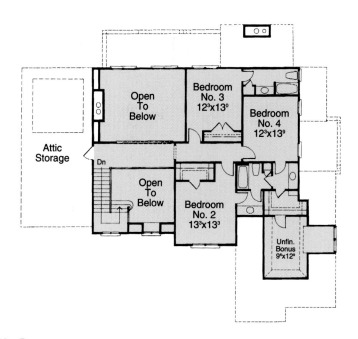

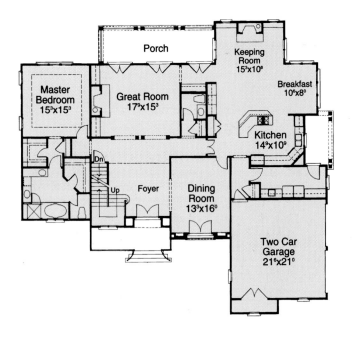

Baronial in attitude, the Chateau style reflects the Renaissance elegance of its namesake castles in France. Here, the basic formality of the Chateau style has been purposely mellowed for modern-day living: the roofline is simplified, and massive masonry construction is replaced by a stucco finish. However, none of the drama has been lost in the translation. The two-story foyer is made for grand entrances, with a marble floor and a sweeping staircase. The foyer opens to the formal dining room and leads to the great room with its fireplace, vaulted ceiling and wet bar. Three sets of double doors open to the rear porch. A fireplace in the quaint keeping room warms the nearby breakfast room, overlooked by the kitchen. Also located on the first floor is the master suite, which provides twin walk-in closets and a pampering bath. Upstairs you will find three generous bedrooms and two baths, one private, plus a bonus room. This home is designed with a walkout basement foundation.

Design HPT220067

First Floor: 1,475 sq. ft.
Second Floor: 1,460 sq. ft.
Total: 2,935 sq. ft.
Width: 57'-6"
Depth: 46'-6"

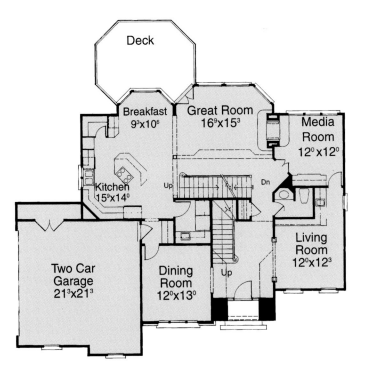

European highlights, such as French shutters, a stucco exterior, arched windows and a double French-door entry that opens to a two-story foyer, all capture the essence of the European Chateau with a few Mediterranean overtones. Inside, the formal dining room on the left offers excellent frontal views, and a formal living room on the right connects to a quaint corner media room. The bayed great room offers access to the rear deck in order to enjoy the full benefits of sun and outdoor activities. A large island kitchen with a bayed breakfast nook also overlooks the rear deck. The two-car garage with extra storage completes the first floor. Upstairs, Bedrooms 2 and 3 share a full bath, while Bedroom 4 includes it own bath. The master suite features a bayed sitting area and an exquisite master bath with a wonderful vanity area, a massive walk-in closet and a unique step-up tub. This home is designed with a walkout basement foundation.

Design HPT220068

First Floor: 1,509 sq. ft.
Second Floor: 1,286 sq. ft.
Total: 2,795 sq. ft.
Bonus Room: 538 sq. ft.
Width: 72'-0"
Depth: 42'-0"

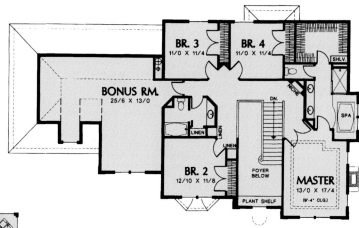

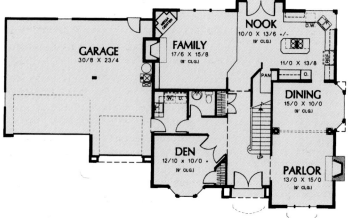

Classic French style brings a touch of *joie de vivre* to this exquisite two-story home. Exterior details such as corner quoins, arches, French shutters and stucco finish lend a European aura to the luxurious silhouette. An enormous arch frames the double-door entry into the home. Space for formal entertaining is shared by the parlor with its warming fireplace and the baronial dining room. An adjacent gourmet kitchen serves the dining room and breakfast nook with equal ease. Enchanting double doors open from the nook to the backyard. The family room features a fireplace, a corner media center and unobstructed views. A laundry room that opens into the garage completes the first floor. The second floor contains four bedrooms, including the grand master suite. Steps away, the master bath with a spa tub invites relaxation. The family bedrooms share a full hall bath. A large bonus room provides additional space for expansion as it is needed.

Design HPT220069

First Floor: 1,961 sq. ft.

Second Floor: 1,472 sq. ft.

Total: 3,433 sq. ft.

Width: 88'-10"

Depth: 47'-2"

D

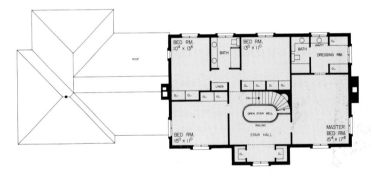

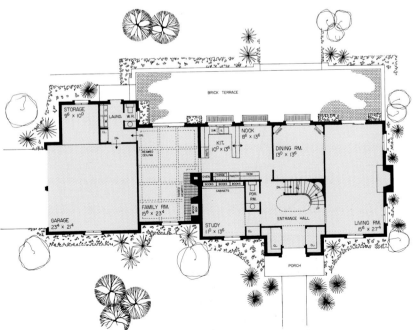

 Stately European magnificence shapes the facade of this elegant brick manor. The formal entrance hall of this French design reveals a cascading curved staircase, which adds to the impressive statement. A spacious living room with a central fireplace makes an ideal location for entertaining, while sliding glass doors access the brick terrace for outdoor livability. To the left, the formal dining room awaits the service of the nearby kitchen, which is placed next to a casual breakfast nook. A beamed ceiling and raised-hearth fireplace accent the family room. The bookshelf-lined study offers a quiet spot for reading. The curving staircase opens to a spacious second-floor stair hall with extra closet space located in the alcove. A master suite provides a fanciful dressing room and private bath. Three additional bedrooms reside on the second floor. A two-car garage with extra storage and a laundry room complete this refined floor plan.

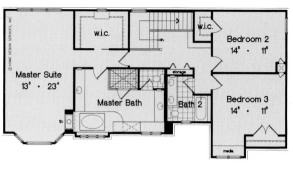

Master Suite
13⁸ · 23⁴

Master Bath

w.i.c.

w.i.c.

Bath 2

storage

Bedroom 2
14⁸ · 11⁸

Bedroom 3
14⁸ · 11⁸

media

Family Rm.
26⁶ · 16¹⁰

Patio
fountain

Nook

Kitchen

Covered Patio

Stor.

storage

wet bar

Laun.

Living Rm.
13¹⁰ · 21⁰

Foyer

Dining Rm.
16² · 13⁰

Rwdr.

w.i.c.

2 Car Garage
23¹⁰ · 24⁴

Entry

Bedroom 4
11⁰ · 11⁰

With lovely European accents, this grand French home speaks the language of elegance. Brick veneer, French shutters and a two-story turret-style bay enlighten this home to a superior level of luxury. A beautiful arch frames the entry into the foyer. To the left, a bayed living room opens through double doors to a rear covered patio. To the right, the formal dining room resides across from the kitchen/nook area. The island kitchen is open to both the nook and spacious family room. The nook opens through double doors onto the rear patio, while the family room warms this area with a cozy fireplace. A bedroom with a walk-in closet is secluded downstairs for a possible guest suite. A laundry room and a two-car garage complete the first floor. Upstairs, the master suite is magnificent and luxurious. A brilliant bay illuminates the bedroom, while the large walk-in closet resides across from the master bath. Bedroom 2 also features a walk-in closet, while Bedroom 3 offers a lovely window seat. These two family bedrooms share a full hall bath.

DESIGN HPT220070

First Floor: 1,971 sq. ft.
Second Floor: 1,482 sq. ft.
Total: 3,453 sq. ft.
Width: 73'-0"
Depth: 62'-0"

GRAND MANORS

"*If I were asked to name the chief benefit of the house, I should say: the house shelters day-dreaming, the house protects the dreamer, the house allows one to dream in peace.*"

—Gaston Bachelard
French philosopher, physicist, mathematician
1884-1962

Photo courtesy of Living Concepts Home Planning

This home, as shown in the photograph, may differ from the actual blueprints.
For more detailed information, please check the floor plans carefully.

DESIGN HPT220071

First Floor: 3,522 sq. ft.
Second Floor: 1,709 sq. ft.
Total: 5,231 sq. ft.
Bonus Space: 274 sq. ft.
Width: 135'-0"
Depth: 87'-8"

Flaring gables and a breezeway highlight the exterior of this grand European-style home. Providing ample space for entertaining, family get-togethers and private moments, this design is hard to beat. The foyer opens into the formal dining room and looks across the hall to the two-story grand room, well named with its central fireplace, bookcases and French doors to the terrace. The gourmet kitchen offers an incredibly large workstation with plenty of counter and cabinet space. Family members will linger over coffee in the morning room and enjoy casual times in the gathering room. The master suite offers private access to the terrace as well as an amenity-laden master bath. A study provides a quiet retreat—or could serve as a home office. The second floor includes four more bedrooms, including one with a private bath. A nearby workshop is one of two in the house—the other, with its own washroom, is between the two garages.

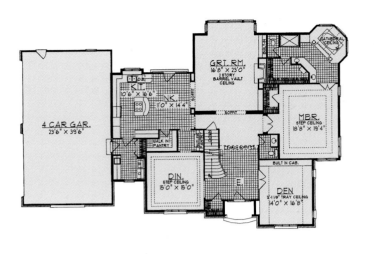

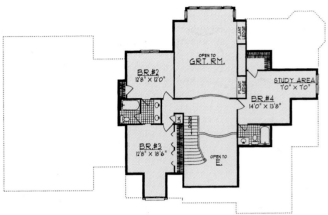

DESIGN HPT220073

First Floor: 3,348 sq. ft.
Second Floor: 2,040 sq. ft.
Total: 5,388 sq. ft.
Bonus Room: 619 sq. ft.
Width: 86'-0"
Depth: 97'-8"

With multiple rooflines accenting the textured look of European-styled stonework, this lavish home starts off on the right foot. Inside, the two-story foyer is flanked by a cozy den to the right and a formal dining room to the left. The den is topped off by a vaulted ceiling and features useful built-in cabinets, while the dining room is topped by a tray ceiling. Directly ahead is the great room, complete with a fireplace and a bayed sitting area. The kitchen is sure to please with a cooktop island and an adjacent nook area for casual meals. A deluxe master bedroom suite on this level assures privacy. Its amenities include two walk-in closets and a sumptuous bath with a bumped-out bayed tub and a cathedral ceiling. An efficient laundry room completes the first floor. Upstairs, two family bedrooms share a full bath, while a third bedroom offers its own bath, making it perfect for a guest suite. A four-car garage will easily shelter the family fleet.

Photo courtesy of Ahmann Designs, Inc.

This home, as shown in the photograph, may differ from the actual blueprints. For more detailed information, please check the floor plans carefully.

Design HPT220074

First Floor: 3,276 sq. ft.
Second Floor: 2,272 sq. ft.
Total: 5,548 sq. ft.
Width: 81'-6"
Depth: 93'-2"

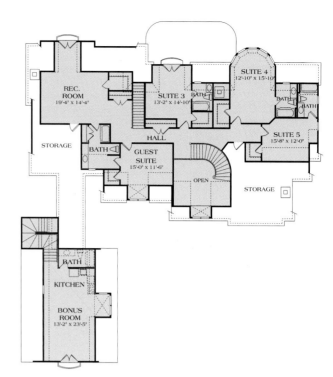

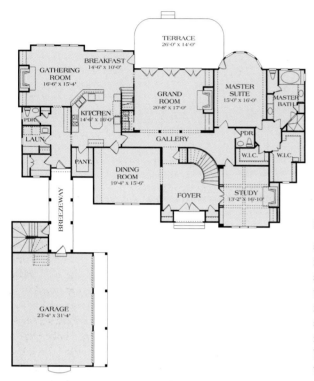

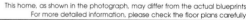

With over 5,000 square feet to work with, this French design uses it all with style and finesse. From the two-story foyer, one can head to the cozy study on the right or view the elegant formal dining room on the left. Directly ahead is the grand room, which easily lives up to its name with a warming fireplace, built-ins and three French doors to the rear terrace. The gourmet of the family will appreciate the openness of the kitchen, with its connections to the sunny breakfast room and nearby gathering room. Located on the first floor for privacy, the master bedroom suite is designed to pamper, with two walk-in closets, a lavish bath and access to the rear terrace. Upstairs, four suites<\m>each with a walk-in closet and private bath<\m>share space with a huge recreation room. Note the large bonus room over the garage; it would make a great studio apartment.

Design HPT220074

First Floor: 3,276 sq. ft.
Second Floor: 2,272 sq. ft.
Total: 5,548 sq. ft.
Width: 81'-6"
Depth: 93'-2"

European decadence reigns free and offers a stately silhouette. This timeless brick exterior showcases slatted shutters and multi-paned, oversized windows. The brick portico with contrasting arches and a balcony adds pizzazz to this sophisticated facade. The designer thoughtfully utilizes space inside and includes many amenities such as a walk-in pantry, an exercise room, numerous built-ins, a computer room and skylights over the screened and covered porches. The foyer introduces a beautiful staircase and is flanked on either side by a study with built-ins and a dining room brightened by a bay window. The family room is warmed by a timeless stone fireplace. A cozy hearth room warms the island countertop kitchen and bayed breakfast room. On the opposite side of the home, the master bedroom features two walk-in closets, linen storage and a vaulted master bath. A rear covered porch, a laundry room, a hobby/exercise room and a split three-car garage with a built-in workbench complete the first floor. Let guests bring their kids along to play in the upstairs game room/home theater! Four additional bedrooms are available for other family members on the second floor. Please specify basement, crawlspace or slab foundation when ordering.

Photo courtesy of Nelson Design Group

This home, as shown in the photograph, may differ from the actual blueprints. For more detailed information, please check the floor plans carefully.

Photo courtesy of Living Concepts Home Planning

This home, as shown in the photograph, may differ from the actual blueprints. For more detailed information, please check the floor plans carefully.

DESIGN HPT220075

First Floor: 1,729 sq. ft.
Second Floor: 2,312 sq. ft.
Total: 4,041 sq. ft.
Width: 71'-6"
Depth: 60'-0"

This dream home is a picturesque vision straight from the French Riviera. Entertaining will be a breeze for the homeowner of this imposing manor. Stucco and French shutters enclose an exquisite European frame. Inside, formal rooms are directly off the foyer, with a powder room nearby. A beautiful staircase cascades down into the formal living room. Family members and friends may prefer the beam-ceilinged gathering room, with its fireplace and access to the covered front terrace. The kitchen, which easily serves both areas, features a walk-in pantry, an island cooktop and a large breakfast nook. Upstairs, the master suite contains a sitting room and access to a private balcony, as well as a sumptuous bath. A reading area is centrally located for all four bedrooms, and a recreation room adds another opportunity for relaxation. A garage with storage and a utility room complete this breathtaking plan.

Photo courtesy of Living Concepts Home Planning

This home, as shown in the photograph, may differ from the actual blueprints. For more detailed information, please check the floor plans carefully.

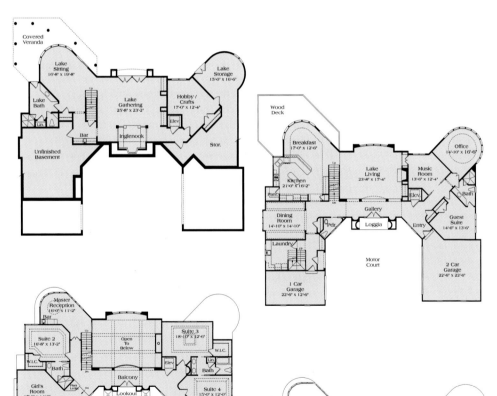

DESIGN HPT220076

First Floor: 2,971 sq. ft.
Second Floor: 2,199 sq. ft.
Third Floor: 1,040 sq. ft.
Finished Basement: 1,707 sq. ft.
Total: 7,917 sq. ft.
Width: 84'-4"
Depth: 64'-11"

Symmetry and stucco present true elegance on the facade of this five-bedroom home and the elegance continues inside over four separate levels. Note the formal and informal gathering areas on the main level: the music room, the lake living room, the formal dining room and the uniquely shaped breakfast room. The second level contains three large bedroom suites—one with its own bath—a spacious girl's room for play time and an entrance room to the third-floor master suite. Lavish is the only way to describe this suite. Complete with His and Hers walk-in closets, a private balcony, an off-season closet and a sumptuous bath, this suite is designed to pamper the homeowner. In the basement is yet more room for casual get-togethers. Note the large sitting room as well as the hobby/crafts room. And tying it all together, an elevator offers stops at each floor.

Design HPT220077

First Floor: 4,002 sq. ft.
Second Floor: 2,338 sq. ft.
Total: 6,340 sq. ft.
Pool House: 2,079 sq. ft.
Width: 133'-4"
Depth: 84'-0"

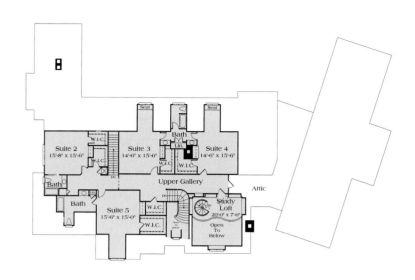

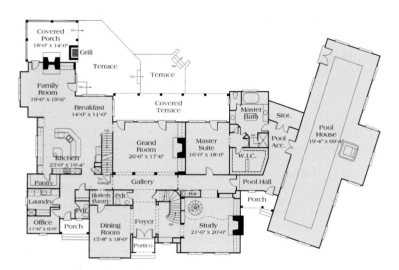

Stonework and shutters on the outside prelude the attractiveness of the interior of this French manor. Flanking the foyer is the formal dining room and two-story study—complete with a fireplace and a spiral staircase to the study loft. The grand room is aptly named, with a second fireplace and direct access to the rear covered terrace. A gallery hall leads to the gourmet island kitchen and breakfast area. A third fireplace is shared with the family room and a covered rear porch with a grill. A lavish master bedroom suite is designed to pamper with a huge double walk-in closet and a luxurious bath offering direct access to the indoor pool! The pool is perfect for swimming laps and getting plenty of exercise in the privacy of your own home. Upstairs, four bedroom suites each feature their own walk-in closet. Bedrooms 3 and 4 share a bath between them, while Bedrooms 2 and 5 offer their own private baths. All of the second-floor bedrooms have access to the study loft.

DESIGN HPT220078

First Floor: 2,439 sq. ft.
Second Floor: 1,934 sq. ft.
Total: 4,373 sq. ft.
Width: 80'-0"
Depth: 55'-0"

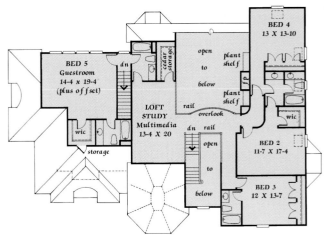

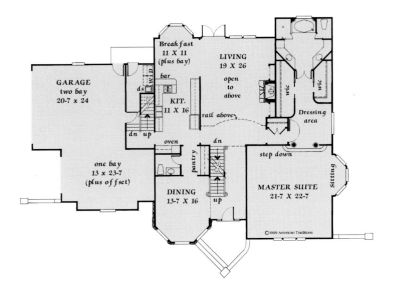

This design is a masterpiece of European styling and French influence. Resembling an old section of the typical European city, this design is enveloped with many medieval features. Picturesque, this home is captured from the quaint narrow streets lined by hipped-roofed brick houses with offsets in the rooflines, large arch-topped windows and delightful flower boxes. Following in this medieval tradition with its characteristic details, this house plan offers intense luxury. The interior is decked out in stately elegance. On the main level, with a dramatic step-down into the master bedroom with a ten-foot ceiling, the master suite is completed with sitting and dressing areas, His and Hers walk-in closets and a spacious spa bath. Back to the entry foyer—columns entice you into the living area of this home. Large bookshelves frame the fireplace and French doors lead to the backyard patio. A formal dining room, a country kitchen and two staircases to the upstairs complete the main floor. On the second floor above the garage, this plan features a private-entry guest room or home office. Above the entry and beyond the curved overlook three additional bedrooms and a loft, multimedia room or study reside.

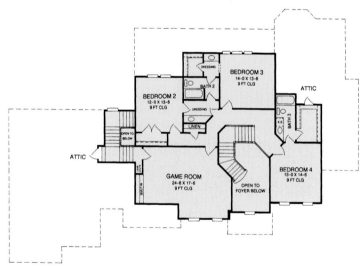

Design HPT220079

First Floor: 2,608 sq. ft.
Second Floor: 1,432 sq. ft.
Total: 4,040 sq. ft.
Width: 89'-10"
Depth: 63'-8"

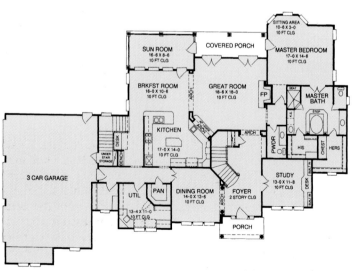

A distinctively French flair is the hallmark of this European-styled home. Stucco, arches and French shutters add to the regal exterior. A classically inspired entrance is framed by timeless columns. Inside, the two-story foyer provides views to the huge great room beyond. A well-placed study off the foyer provides an area for a useful home office. The kitchen, breakfast room and sun room are adjacent and lend a spacious feel. The great room is visible from this area through decorative arches. A roomy utility room receives laundry from a chute above. A nearby built-in bench and desk help organize the rear entry of the home. The master suite includes a roomy sitting area and a lovely master bath with a centerpiece whirlpool tub flanked by half-columns. Upstairs, Bedrooms 2 and 3 share a bath that includes private dressing areas, while Bedroom 4 accesses a private bath. An enormous game room is located upstairs and is reached by the convenient rear stair. Please specify crawlspace or slab foundation when ordering.

DESIGN HPT220080

First Floor: 3,261 sq. ft.
Second Floor: 1,920 sq. ft.
Total: 5,181 sq. ft.
Optional Basement: 710 sq. ft.
Width: 86'-2"
Depth: 66'-10"

Elegantly styled in the French countryside tradition, this home features a well-thought-out floor plan with all the amenities. Stucco and stone and French shutters grace the exterior. A large dining room and a study open off the two-story grand foyer that showcases a lovely flared staircase. A covered patio is accessed from the large formal living room. A more informal family room is conveniently located off the kitchen and breakfast room. The roomy master suite includes a sitting area, a luxurious private bath and its own entrance to the study. The second floor can be reached from the formal front staircase or a well-placed rear staircase. Three large bedrooms and a game room are located upstairs. Bedrooms 3 and 4 feature private dressing areas and a shared bath. Bedroom 2 shares a bath with the game room. The walkout basement can be expanded to provide more living space. Please specify basement or crawlspace foundation when ordering.

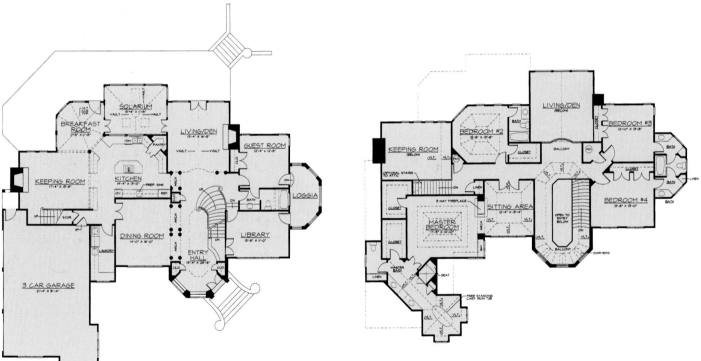

Design HPT22008I

First Floor: 2,425 sq. ft.

Second Floor: 2,090 sq. ft.

Total: 4,515 sq. ft.

Width: 80'-0"

Depth: 67'-0"

This French estate home is impressive with a beautiful castle-like turret. Inside, spacious rooms will easily accommodate life's diverse pattern of formal occasions and casual times. The entry is impressive enough with an immaculate staircase spiraling to the second floor. A dining room is found to the left, framed by columns and archways. A sophisticated library accesses a loggia shared with the guest bedroom. The two-story living room is warmed by an enormous hearth and overlooked by a romantic second-floor balcony. Skylights and terrace access highlight the solarium, while the island kitchen easily serves the breakfast room. Casual areas are kept intimate in the two-story keeping room warmed by a fireplace. A set of double doors gives entry to the vaulted sitting room of the second-floor master suite. An arch leads to the bedroom warmed by a three-way fireplace. The suite is further enhanced by His and Hers walk-in closets and a vaulted bath.

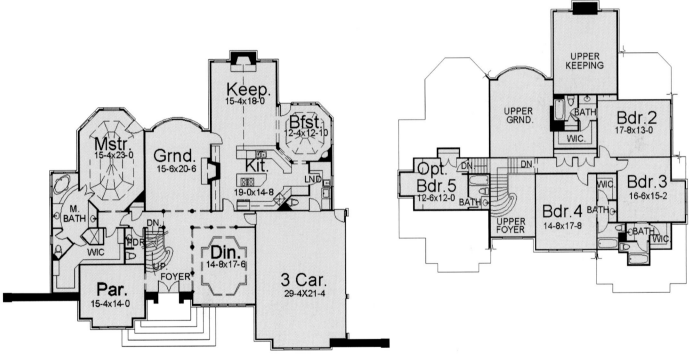

DESIGN HPT220082

First Floor: 2,670 sq. ft.
Second Floor: 1,255 sq. ft.
Total: 3,925 sq. ft.
Width: 70'-6"
Depth: 66'-6"

European extravagance, dazzled with chateau style, makes this enormous manor home the epitome of luxury and charm. A dramatic display of windows and a glorious arched entrance beautify the exterior. Stately steps lead up the front porch to double doors, which open inside to the spacious two-story foyer. A dramatic staircase cascades into foyer, which is flanked on either side by the formal dining room and parlor. The dining room is defined by its outlying columns. Straight ahead, the lofty two-story grand room is illuminated by a curved wall of windows at the rear. An enormous hearth warms the entire room and is flanked by built-in shelves. The cozy keeping room, warmed by a second fireplace, is open to both the casual bayed breakfast room and the gourmet island kitchen. The three-car garage is located nearby. The left wing of the main floor is almost entirely devoted to the master suite, which provides a large master bath with a whirlpool tub and a huge walk-in closet. Upstairs, all of the family bedrooms feature their own private baths. The optional fifth bedroom can also be converted to a home office and has a private bath.

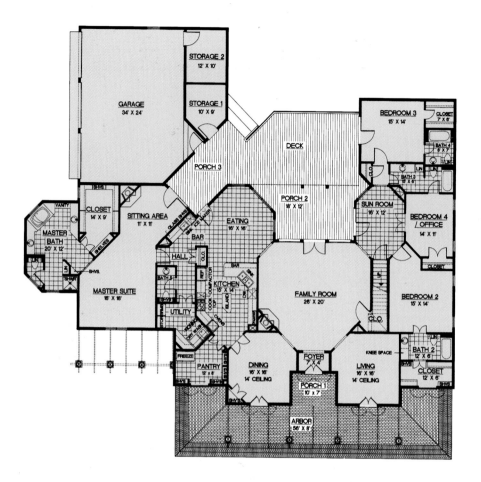

DESIGN HPT220083

Square Footage: 3,960
Width: 96'-0"
Depth: 90'-0"

Opulence and extreme luxury are the themes of this European dream. This home will make a bold statement in any neighborhood. A one-of-a-kind French design, this plan boasts varying levels of hipped rooflines, columns, shuttered windows and a large front arbor/porch. A foyer leads into the spacious family room, complete with a fireplace, while the dining room and living room flank the foyer. The kitchen area is comprised of an eating space, pantry and utility area—all of which are tiled. A large porch/deck area graces the rear of the house, and a sun room allows for plenty of lazy afternoons basking in the warmth. The decadent master suite boasts glass shelves and a sitting area with a fireplace, while additional shelves are found in the walk-in closet. Three additional bedrooms each have their own full bath. Two large storage areas positioned near the three-car garage complete this plan. Please specify basement, crawlspace or slab foundation when ordering.

Design HPT220084

First Floor: 2,006 sq. ft.
Second Floor: 1,799 sq. ft.
Total: 3,805 sq. ft.
Width: 71'-8"
Depth: 54'-2"

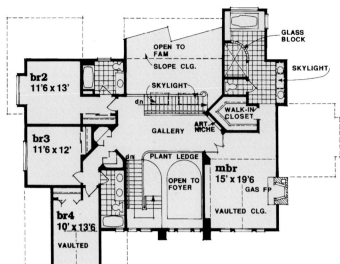

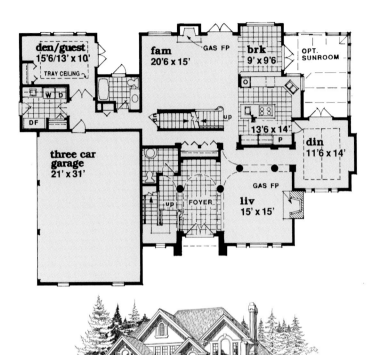

Alternate Elevation

This beautifully detailed, luxurious four-bedroom home offers an exterior of traditional brick. An optional stucco elevation is also available. A high arched entrance makes a dramatic first impression. The two-story foyer opens to an impressive colonnade, creating a regal entry into this exclusive European home. The pillars visually separate the living room, main foyer and hallway. The spacious kitchen, with a center cooking island, offers a large breakfast bar and corner sink overlooking the optional sun room. A private den or guest room with an adjacent full bath provides rear access through double French doors. A railed gallery opens to the vaulted family room and the main foyer creates privacy for the master bedroom retreat. The elegant master bath features a skylit twin vanity, a large shower, a soaking tub and a compartmented toilet. A secondary rear stairway provides access to the three family bedrooms. A three-car garage and a utility room are useful additions to this family charmer.

Design HPT220085

First Floor: 2,182 sq. ft.
Second Floor: 856 sq. ft.
Total: 3,038 sq. ft.
Width: 62'-0"
Depth: 54'-0"

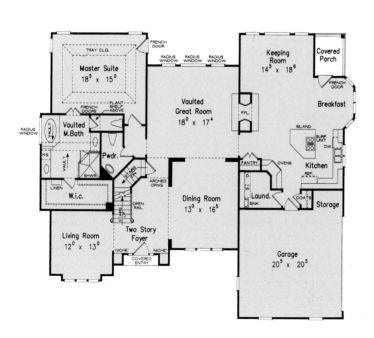

Arched windows, shutters and lintels add a touch of European flavor to this two-story, four-bedroom home. The covered entry gives way to a spectacular two-story foyer that introduces a cascading staircase from the second floor. To the left is a formal living room, and to the right a spacious dining area—perfect for elegant occasions. The vaulted great room is immense, and includes a see-through fireplace to the cooktop-island kitchen and the keeping room. Three radius windows illuminate the interior. A bayed breakfast area—accessible to a covered porch—is also included in this area of the home. The master bedroom features a tray ceiling and French doors opening to a luxurious private bath and a vast walk-in closet. Upstairs, each family bedroom is complete with individual walk-in closets—one bedroom also contains a private full bath. Please specify basement or crawlspace foundation when ordering.

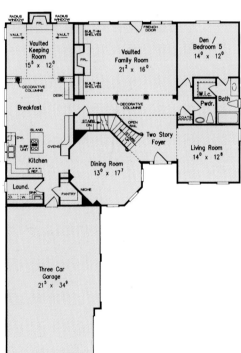

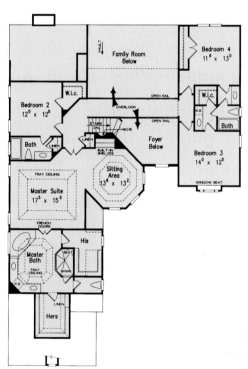

Design HPT220086

First Floor: 2,060 sq. ft.

Second Floor: 1,817 sq. ft.

Total: 3,877 sq. ft.

Width: 54'-0"

Depth: 78'-4"

Mesmerizing features make this luxurious mansion a distinct sensation. Stucco and stone, opulent arches and French shutters romanticize the exterior of its blissful perfection. Inside, a radiant staircase cascades into the two-story foyer. The eye-catching stone turret encloses the dining room. The formal living room is illuminated by two enormous arched windows. A wall of windows in the great room offers a breathtaking view of the backyard. Vaulted ceilings add an open, airy feeling to the keeping and family rooms, which are warmed by fireplaces. The island kitchen adjoins the breakfast area and a walk-in pantry. A three-car garage completes the ground level. Upstairs, the master wing is almost doubled by its private sitting area. Double doors open into the master bath with a corner whirlpool tub, separate glass shower, double vanities and a compartmented toilet. Enormous His and Hers walk-in closets are efficiently designed. Bedroom 2 offers its own private bath, while Bedrooms 3 and 4 share a bath between them. Please specify basement or crawlspace foundation when ordering.

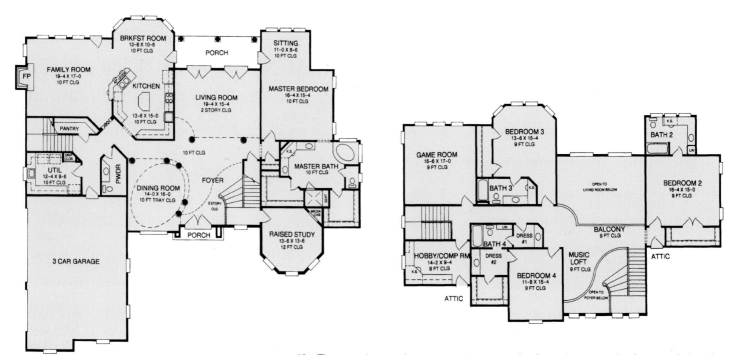

DESIGN HPT220087

First Floor: 3,058 sq. ft.
Second Floor: 2,076 sq. ft.
Total: 5,134 sq. ft.
Width: 79'-6"
Depth: 73'-10"

Right out of *Beauty and the Beast*, this fairy tale manor glorifies French decadence and European architecture. A series of hipped roofs and a castle-style turret create a magical silhouette. Brick and stone complement the formal exterior, and a grand arch frames the doorway. Double doors open into a lofty foyer, which faces a cascading staircase with palatial elegance. To the left, an oval dining room is outlined by formal columns. Straight ahead, two columns frame the formal living room that offers two sets of doors to the rear porch. The island kitchen is open to the breakfast room that accesses the rear porch. The family room is enhanced by a wall of glass and features a warming fireplace. The master wing offers a sitting area and a master bath with two walk-in closets. A sophisticated raised study is a quiet retreat. Upstairs, a romantic balcony overlooks the living room and extends to a music loft. All of the family bedrooms on the second floor offer their own baths. A hobby room with built-ins resides across from the game room. A rear stairway leads down to a utility room and garage. Please specify basement, crawlspace or slab foundation when ordering.

DESIGN HPT220088

First Floor: 2,384 sq. ft.
Second Floor: 1,234 sq. ft.
Total: 3,618 sq. ft.
Bonus Room: 314 sq. ft.
Width: 64'-6"
Depth: 57'-10"

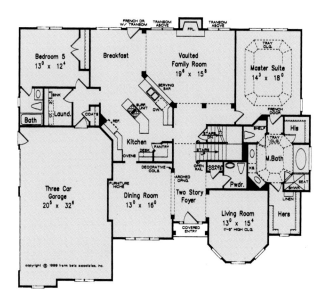

French details combine with the intermingled influences of European style to present a manor bursting with amenities. Stucco and stone, French shutters, a turret-style bay and lovely arches create a magical timeless style. A formal arch romanticizes the front entry, which opens into a two-story foyer. A bayed living room resides to the right, while a formal dining room is set to the left. Straight ahead, the vaulted two-story family room is warmed by an enchanting fireplace. The island workstation kitchen is set between the breakfast and dining rooms. The master suite is enhanced by a tray ceiling and offers a lavish master bath with a whirlpool tub, separate shower, double vanities, a compartmented toilet and His and Hers walk-in closets. A family bedroom on the opposite side of the first floor features a private bath and would make a perfect guest suite. A nearby laundry room resides on the way to the three-car garage. Upstairs, Bedroom 2 offers another private bath and a walk-in closet. Bedrooms 3 and 4 each provide their own walk-in closet and share a full bath between them. The optional bonus room will make a great home office or playroom. Please specify basement or crawlspace foundation when ordering.

DESIGN HPT220089

First Floor: 3,520 sq. ft.
Second Floor: 1,638 sq. ft.
Total: 5,158 sq. ft.
Bonus Room: 411 sq. ft.
Width: 96'-6"
Depth: 58'-8"

This custom-designed estate home elegantly combines stone and stucco, arched windows and stunning exterior details under its formidable hipped roof. Front-porch columns frame the double-door entry into the home. Inside, the two-story foyer is impressive with its grand staircase, tray ceiling and overlooking balcony. An elegant dining room and a sophisticated library flank the foyer on either side. Equally remarkable is the generous living room with a fireplace and a coffered two-story ceiling. The island kitchen, breakfast bay and family room with a fireplace are all open to one another for a comfortable, casual atmosphere. The first-floor master suite indulges with numerous closets, a dressing room and a fabulous bath. Upstairs, four more bedrooms are topped by tray ceilings—three have walk-in closets and two have private baths. The three-car garage boasts additional storage and a bonus room above. The bonus room would make a wonderful guest suite, playroom or quiet home office for future use.

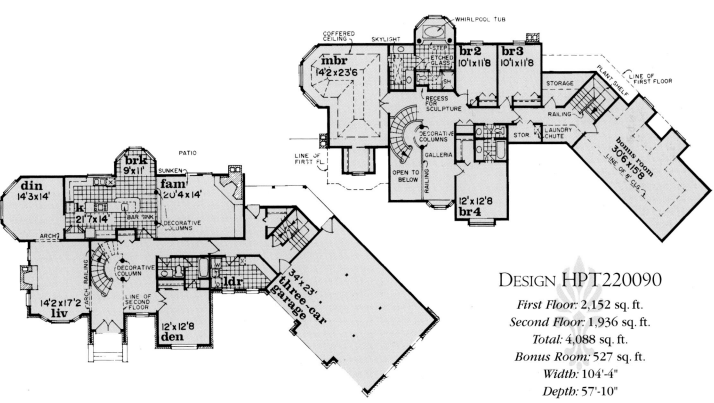

COFFERED CEILING

SKYLIGHT

WHIRLPOOL TUB

mbr 14'2 x 23'6

STEP ETCHED GLASS

SH

RECESS FOR SCULPTURE

br2 10'1 x 11'8

br3 10'1 x 11'8

STORAGE

LINE OF FIRST FLOOR

PLANT SHELF

RAILING

LAUNDRY CHUTE

STOR.

bonus room 30'6 x 15'8 LINE OF 8' CLG

DECORATIVE COLUMNS

LINE OF FIRST FL.

GALLERIA

OPEN TO BELOW

RAILING

br4 12' x 12'8

PATIO

brk 9' x 11'

SUNKEN

fam 20'4 x 14'

DECORATIVE COLUMNS

BAR SINK

din 14'3 x 14'

k 21'7 x 14'

ARCH?

DECORATIVE COLUMN

ARCH RAILING

liv 14'2 x 17'2

LINE OF SECOND FLOOR

ldr

three-car garage 34' x 23'

den 12' x 12'8

DESIGN HPT220090

First Floor: 2,152 sq. ft.

Second Floor: 1,936 sq. ft.

Total: 4,088 sq. ft.

Bonus Room: 527 sq. ft.

Width: 104'-4"

Depth: 57'-10"

In elegant Tudor style, this French estate home offers all of the best of luxury living. The vaulted foyer introduces a circular staircase and a gallery above. The living room with its bay window and fireplace is on the left; a cozy den with double-door access is on the right. The dining room is defined by an arched opening and also features a bay window. The U-shaped kitchen features a bar sink and bayed breakfast nook. Enter the sunken family room through decorative columns. You'll find a corner fireplace and sliding glass doors to the rear yard. The second floor holds four bedrooms, one of which is a master suite with a coffered ceiling and private bath. Family bedrooms share a full bath. Bedroom 4 offers a walk-in closet. A bonus room just beyond the secondary staircase allows for 527 square feet of future space. A large three-car garage completes this plan.

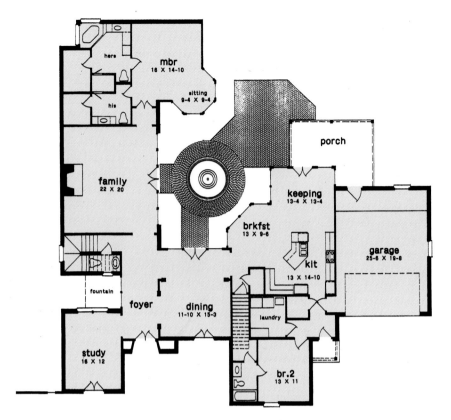

DESIGN HPT220091

First Floor: 2,929 sq. ft.
Second Floor: 1,262 sq. ft.
Total: 4,191 sq. ft.
Width: 79'-6"
Depth: 77'-4"

Classical Old World styling with a steeply pitched roof, shuttered windows and dormers will make this home the envy of every neighborhood. An arched doorway opens into the foyer, which is flanked on either side by the study on the left and the dining room on the right. An enormous fireplace warms the cozy family room with an enchanting view. The magical highlight of this design is the rear courtyard with a fountain that opens from the family and dining rooms—and it can be seen from the bayed sitting area in the master suite. Here, the master suite boasts unquestionable luxury—His and Hers bathrooms and walk-in closets provide lavish privacy. The quiet study on the first floor and a sizable game room upstairs are among the special features in this home. Split bedrooms and a large gathering area consisting of the breakfast nook, keeping room and kitchen satisfy both privacy and family demands.

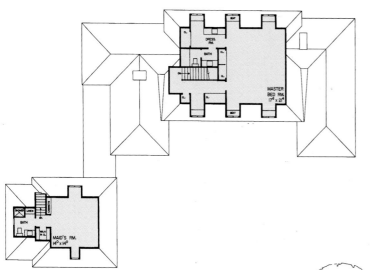

Design HPT220092

First Floor: 2,658 sq. ft.
Second Floor: 1,216 sq. ft.
Total: 3,874 sq. ft.
Width: 104'-5"
Depth: 72'-10"

L

The elegance of pleasing proportion and delightful detailing has seldom been better exemplified than by this classic French country manor adaptation. Build as a one-story home to begin with, then later finish the master suite and the maid's suite, which is located over the garage. The main level contains plenty of livability with a gigantic living room, nearby dining room and cozy library. Special features make these living areas a treat: a warming fireplace, sliding glass doors to the rear terrace and built-ins. A family room is located at the end of the hall and offers its own fireplace. Two bedrooms at the opposite end of the hall share a full bath that includes double vanities and a separate tub and shower. If you choose to finish the master suite, you'll discover its delights: window seats in the dormers, a dressing area with a sink, five closets and a full bath. The maid's quarters might make a fine guest suite. Note the huge garden storage area outside the two-car garage.

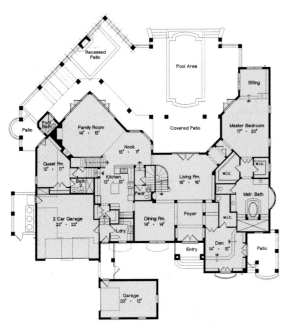

A gentle blend of European flavors lends multi-cultural styles and breathtaking elegance to this timeless design. Sweeping verandas, a grand two-story entry and intricate balustrades borrow freely from the alluring French countryside, with a dash of Mediterranean spice. Outstanding architectural details are enhanced by the use of cast stone, balustrades, ornamental iron and stone. This mesmerizing facade and other splendid features are reminiscent of days gone by. The entry is rich with architectural details: a twenty-foot ceiling and three "Juliet" balconies. Walls of glass and soaring ceilings create a spacious atmosphere. A quiet den can double as a home office for the entrepreneur. The living room hosts an enchanting curved stairway and opens to the patio and pool area. The master suite offers serene views in the sitting area, which acts as a sumptuous reading retreat. Two walk-in closets are offered, as well as a luxuriously styled master bath with a central whirlpool tub and a bumped-out window view. The master suite also accesses the patio, which lays claim to a lagoon-style pool with a sandbar, spa, waterfall and fountain. Garden courtyards off the study and dining room gracefully complete the main level. Upstairs, two family bedrooms share a bath.

DESIGN HPT220093

First Floor: 3,517 sq. ft.
Second Floor: 1,254 sq. ft.
Total: 4,771 sq. ft.
Width: 95'-8"
Depth: 107'-0"

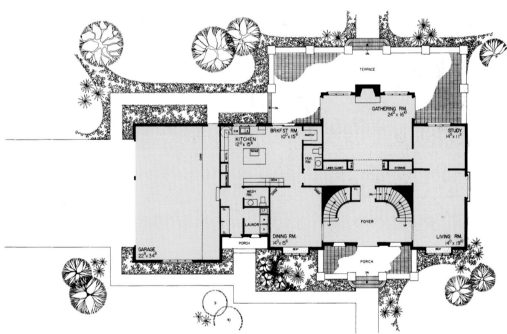

DESIGN HPT220094

First Floor: 2,345 sq. ft.
Second Floor: 1,687 sq. ft.
Total: 4,032 sq. ft.
Width: 90'-4"
Depth: 44'-0"

L D

This best-selling French adaptation is highlighted by effective window treatments, delicate cornice detailing, appealing brick quoins and excellent proportions. Stately symmetry enhances the formal look of the exterior. Inside, a large two-story foyer leads under the arch of a dual staircase to a gathering room graced by a central fireplace and access to the rear terrace. The formal living and dining rooms flank the foyer and work well together for entertaining. The gourmet kitchen offers a work island and features an attached breakfast room with a huge walk-in pantry and access to the terrace. Upstairs, a deluxe master bedroom suite is lavish in its efforts to pamper you. The dressing room offers a walk-in closet, while the master bath offers double vanities. Three secondary bedrooms share this level: one has its own bath and a walk-in closet while two others share a full hall bath. A spacious garage completes this plan.

Everything you remember about French Chateau architecture is part of this magnificent estate home. From the opulent towers to the porte cochere—this is palatial living! An oversized front entry beckons your attention to the wonderful amenities inside: a raised, marble vestibule with a circular stair; a formal library and dining hall with views to the veranda and pool beyond; and a family gathering hall, open to the kitchen and connected to the outdoor grill. The master suite is embellished with a nature garden, His and Hers wardrobes, a fireplace and an elegant bath. The second floor offers more living space; a media presentation room and game room. Each of the family bedrooms features a private bath—one suite is reached via a bridge over the porte cochere. Other unique details include a wet bar in the game area, a sunset balcony, and a dual-use butler's pantry with a motorized screen to hide the bar pass-through to the reception hall and herb garden.

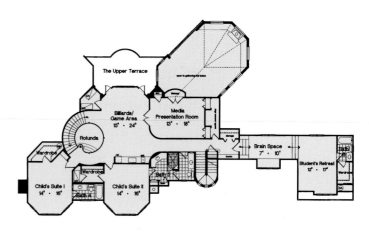

DESIGN HPT220095

First Floor: 3,588 sq. ft.
Second Floor: 2,062 sq. ft.
Total: 5,650 sq. ft.
Width: 137'-8"
Depth: 91'-7"

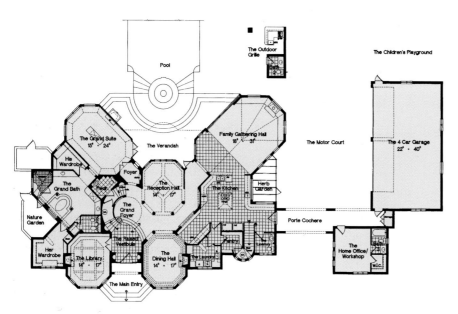

DESIGN HPT220096

First Floor: 2,553 sq. ft.
Second Floor: 1,370 sq. ft.
Total: 3,923 sq. ft.
Width: 74'-0"
Depth: 99'-4"

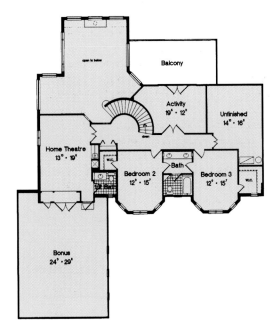

The castle-like facade of this romantic fairy tale home encloses a floor plan fit for royalty. Dazzling turrets, French accents and a stately presence give this home a dramatic European appeal. The entry leads inside to a foyer flanked on either side by a den/office and a formal dining room. A curved staircase is placed behind the living room, which overlooks the rear porch. The master suite features a spacious sitting area and a lavish bath that includes two vanities, His and Hers walk-in closets, an oval tub and a separate shower. Casual areas of the home include the kitchen overlooking the breakfast nook and the open two-story family room with a warming fireplace. The family room accesses the rear covered porch, while the breakfast nook connects to a side patio. Upstairs, Bedrooms 2 and 3 with walk-in closets share a bath. An unfinished room at the end of the hall is great for a fourth bedroom or home office. Double doors open into an activity room that accesses a balcony. The home theater accesses an enormous bonus room.

DESIGN HPT220097

First Floor: 4,351 sq. ft.

Second Floor: 3,534 sq. ft.

Total: 7,885 sq. ft.

Bonus Room: 780 sq. ft.

Width: 132'-0"

Depth: 75'-0"

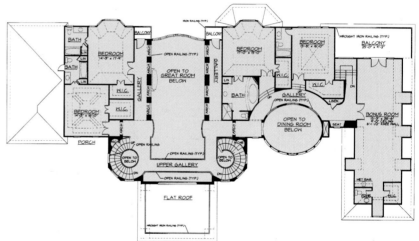

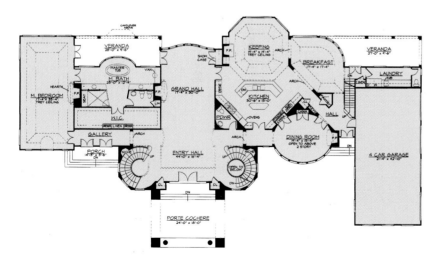

You can almost hear the horses' hooves trotting along as they draw up to the porte cochere, depositing party-goers to the delights of this fine European estate. Resembling a historic estate home in France, this version was adapted to make even the fussiest homeowner of the modern-day world comfortable. The entry hall and grand hall are melded into one huge reception area, waiting for arriving guests. Serve formal dinners in the oval dining room with glass surrounding one whole side. The keeping room boasts a more casual atmosphere, but is decorated with a dazzling tray ceiling as accent. A gallery leads to the master suite, which also offers a tray ceiling, plus private access to a rear veranda. The master bath is a pampering haven, and provides access to a lavish walk-in closet. The second floor holds four secondary bedroom suites and an enormous bonus room to develop as needs arise. Don't miss the four-car garage at the right side of the plan.

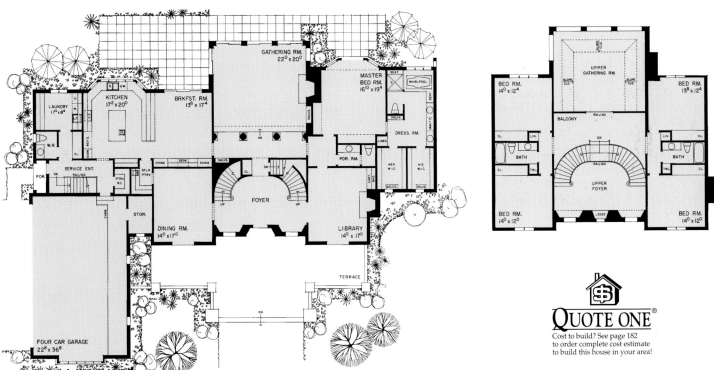

Quote One®

Cost to build? See page 182
to order complete cost estimate
to build this house in your area!

DESIGN HPT220098

First Floor: 3,350 sq. ft.
Second Floor: 1,298 sq. ft.
Total: 4,648 sq. ft.
Width: 97'-0"
Depth: 74'-4"

Reminiscent of a Mediterranean villa, this grand manor is a showstopper on the outside and a comfortable residence on the inside. Corner quoins, a stucco finish, arched windows and French shutters combine to give the exterior a stately European appearance. Inside, an elegant receiving hall boasts a double staircase and is flanked by the formal dining room and the library. A huge gathering room is found to the rear and is graced by a fireplace and a wall of sliding glass doors to the rear terrace. The large island workstation kitchen resides next to an informal breakfast area. The master bedroom is found on the first floor for privacy. With a lavish bath to pamper you, and His and Hers walk-in closets, this suite will be a delight to retire to each evening. A four-car garage completes the first floor. Upstairs are four additional bedrooms with ample storage space, a large balcony overlooking the gathering room and two full baths.

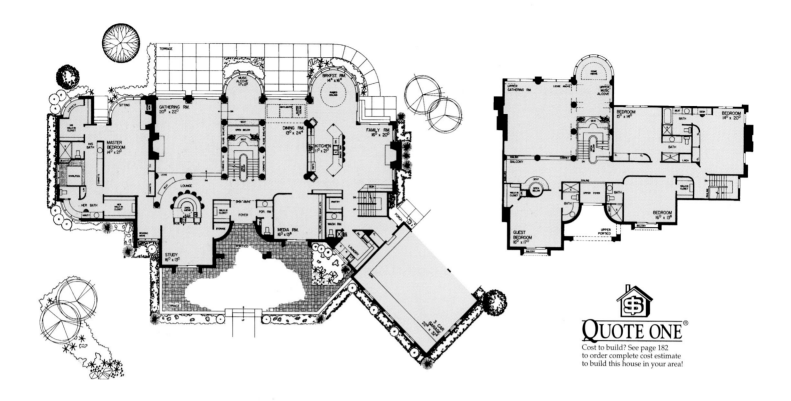

DESIGN HPT220099

First Floor: 4,786 sq. ft.
Second Floor: 1,842 sq. ft.
Total: 6,628 sq. ft.
Width: 133'-8"
Depth: 87'-10"

L D

Graceful window arches soften the massive chimneys and hipped roof of this grand European manor that's dazzled with French highlights. Inside, a two-story gathering room is just two steps down from the adjacent lounge with an impressive wet bar and a semi-circular music alcove. This area is reserved for elegant entertaining or decadent relaxation. The highly efficient galley-style kitchen overlooks the family-room fireplace and spectacular windowed breakfast room. The rear terrace is perfect for outdoor entertaining. The master suite is a private retreat with a fireplace and a wood box tucked into the corner of its sitting room. Separate His and Hers baths and dressing rooms guarantee plenty of space and privacy. A large, built-in whirlpool tub adds the final touch. A garage and utility room make the floor plan more efficient. Upstairs, a second-floor balcony overlooks the gathering room below. There are also four additional bedrooms, each with a private bath.

QUOTE ONE®
Cost to build? See page 182
to order complete cost estimate
to build this house in your area!

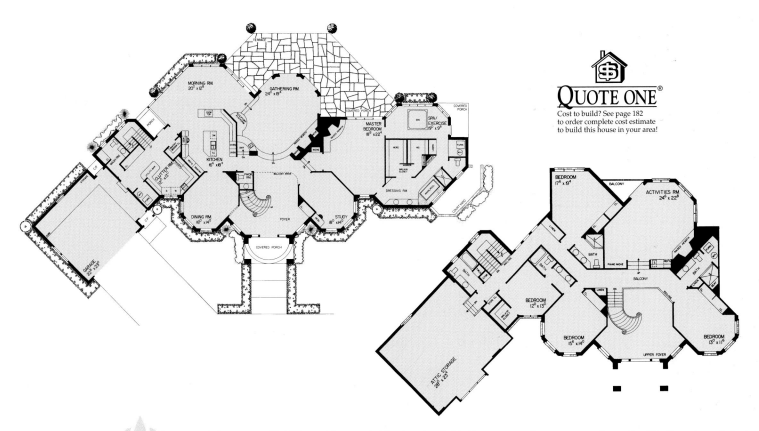

DESIGN HPT220100

First Floor: 3,736 sq. ft.
Second Floor: 2,264 sq. ft.
Total: 6,000 sq. ft.
Width: 133'-4"
Depth: 65'-5"

L

The castle-like facade of this European-style manor speaks well of its French roots but sparkles with a fresh personality. Sunburst fanlights set off historic elements such as Romanesque arches and massive turrets, while organic shades of brick meld with the landscape. An enticing simplicity decorates the home, inside and out, and the entire interior flows with an easy panache and timeless spirit. Honey-hued hardwood adds warmth to alabaster-toned walls and ceilings throughout the interior. Arch-topped windows and skylights splash the indoors with wide views of nature and light, which, when mixed with the French-inspired architecture, create a sense of romance and individuality. The plan opens to a dining room and a step-down gathering room, which features a raised-hearth fireplace. A study occupies the base of the right turret. The kitchen includes an island workstation. Windows and skylights brighten the eating area, while glass doors lead out to the terrace. The master bedroom offers a sitting area with a fireplace and a triple window, which looks out to the terrace. The suite features a deluxe spa and exercise room. The upstairs includes four bedrooms and an activities room that offers a piano niche, morning kitchen and fireplace. A triangular balcony overlooks the terrace.

LANDSCAPES

"Art is the unceasing effort to compete with the beauty of flowers—and never succeeding"
—Marc Chagall
Russian-born French painter
1887-1985

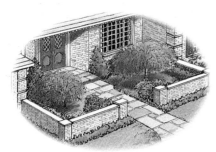

The walled courtyard garden featured in this design creates a formal entrance in keeping with the elegant architecture. Sweeping lines used in the planting beds and driveway carry the eye past the house on the other end, complementing the low lines of the house.

FRENCH COUNTRY RAMBLER

This country French home has elegant horizontal lines and a symmetrical facade that the designer accentuates with the long lines of the drive, lawn and walkway. The elongated, narrow lawn panel in front of the house continues past the corner tree, giving the impression of a long, sweeping vista. A circular driveway is not used in this plan, yet to make provision for adequate parking near the front door, a parking spur was added. An exquisite weeping tree accents the horizontal sight line from the parking spur and directs the eye toward the front door. This elegant tree is also the first thing seen upon leaving the front door.

Large evergreens screen the garage and rear parking areas as well as provide landscape interest, color and texture. These are balanced at the other side of the house by a tall flowering tree, which is a surprise addition to the otherwise symmetrical planting scheme. A small inner courtyard at the front door greets visitors and creates a transition from semi-public to private space. Defined by a low brick wall, the courtyard features symmetrically placed shrubs and a pair of ornamental trees, in keeping with the sophisticated ambiance of the house.

Design HPT220101

Shown in Summer
Design by Michael J. Opisso

PLAN VIEW

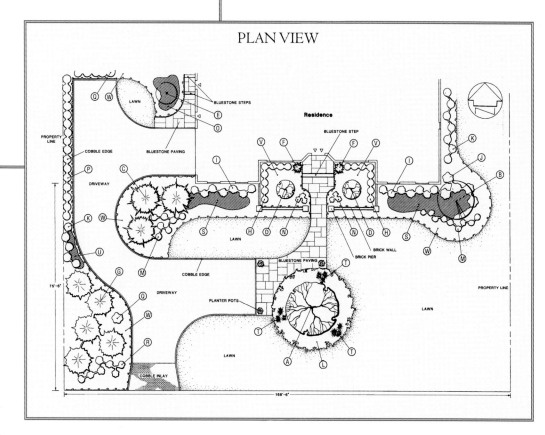

REGIONALIZED PLANT LISTS

Because climate and growing conditions vary greatly throughout North America, it is impossible to list here specific plants for this landscape plan that would thrive in all regions of the country. However, you can order a Blueprint Package for this plan containing a list of plants selected by experts for your region.

The six-page Blueprint Package features a large-size version of this Plan View, plus a detailed Plant and Materials List. It also includes an illustrated list of hundreds of landscape plants suited to your region, to use if you wish to make substitutions, as well as planting instructions and plant adaptation maps to ensure professional-looking results.

See page 184 to order your regionalized Blueprint Package.

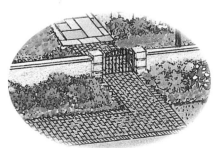

Lots of trees and large shrubs endow a suburban lot with the mood of a French country estate. To minimize pruning, the plants are carefully chosen for their upright shape, compact growth and ability to stay within bounds over the years.

CHARMING COUNTRY ESTATE

An abundance of trees and shrubs surrounds this French country home, making it look more like a private, wooded estate in Europe rather than a suburban lot in New York, Iowa or California. The flowering deciduous trees lined up along the front of the property are repeated near the entrance, leading your eye toward the front door. A single tree with an elegant weeping form and purple foliage provides an accent near the extension at the back of the house, and creates a focal point from the driveway entrance.

Some aspects of formality, while creating the grand look demanded by the architecture, are modified for ease of care. For instance, the dense, upright conifers set in a neat row along the driveway are allowed to grow naturally instead of being clipped into a formal hedge, which would require more labor. On the opposite side of the property, a staggered row of narrow conifers is also spaced for minimum pruning. The smooth expanse of green grass at the front of the lot gives the illusion that the house sits farther back than it really does, yet it is small enough to maintain without professional help.

A house this size needs plenty of parking space for family and friends. The designer breaks up the large expanse of driveway with decorative brick inlays and with a planting peninsula, which shields the garage from direct view. A parking bay near the front walk provides convenient parking for visitors, who can stroll right up the front walk toward the secluded entry courtyard after getting out of their cars.

DESIGN HPT220102

SHOWN IN SPRING
Design by Salvatore A. Masullo

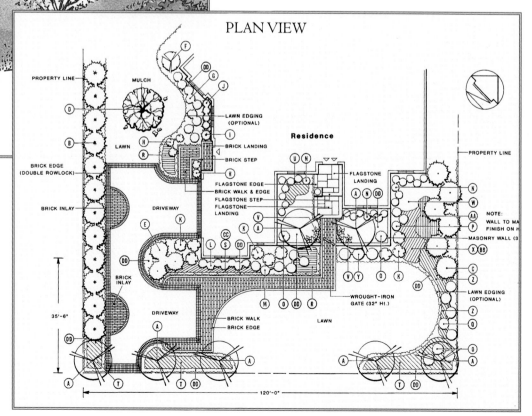

PLAN VIEW

REGIONALIZED PLANT LISTS

Because climate and growing conditions vary greatly throughout North America, it is impossible to list here specific plants for this landscape plan that would thrive in all regions of the country. However, you can order a Blueprint Package for this plan containing a list of plants selected by experts for your region.

The six-page Blueprint Package features a large-size version of this Plan View, plus a detailed Plant and Materials List. It also includes an illustrated list of hundreds of landscape plants suited to your region, to use if you wish to make substitutions, as well as planting instructions and plant adaptation maps to ensure professional-looking results.

See page 184 to order your regionalized Blueprint Package.

EUROPEAN FLAIR

The designer uses graceful curving borders to bring this landscape to life. An appealing mix of shrubs grown for their ornamental foliage, flowers and fruit rises form an underplanting of weed-smothering groundcovers and long-blooming perennials. The shrubs' compact growth habits keep the windows clear and save on pruning chores. A small tree, selected for its handsome branching pattern and long season of colorful foliage, partially screens the entry from public view and creates a dramatic focal point. The curves in the borders are repeated in the cobble-edged planting peninsulas, which visually break up the large expanse of asphalt in the drive.

Five deciduous shade trees planted along the drive spruce up this utilitarian area while giving needed height to the landscape. The trees are chosen for their airy canopies of delicate leaves, which create a softening screen without excessive shade or fall cleanup. A flagstone walk, set in concrete and mortared for weed-free maintenance, zigzags from the drive to the front porch. For a greater feeling of privacy, the designer ends the walk short of the street so that it is accessible only from the drive. The curving borders jut into the lawn, giving it an appealing shape—and a size that isn't too large for the easy-care gardener to handle comfortably. The lawn is kept free of plantings and other obstacles to make mowing faster and easier.

DESIGN HPT220103

SHOWN IN SPRING
Design by Edward D. Georges

REGIONALIZED PLANT LISTS

Because climate and growing conditions vary greatly throughout North America, it is impossible to list here specific plants for this landscape plan that would thrive in all regions of the country. However, you can order a Blueprint Package for this plan containing a list of plants selected by experts for your region.

The six-page Blueprint Package features a large-size version of this Plan View, plus a detailed Plant and Materials List. It also includes an illustrated list of hundreds of landscape plants suited to your region, to use if you wish to make substitutions, as well as planting instructions and plant adaptation maps to ensure professional-looking results.

See page 184 to order your regionalized Blueprint Package.

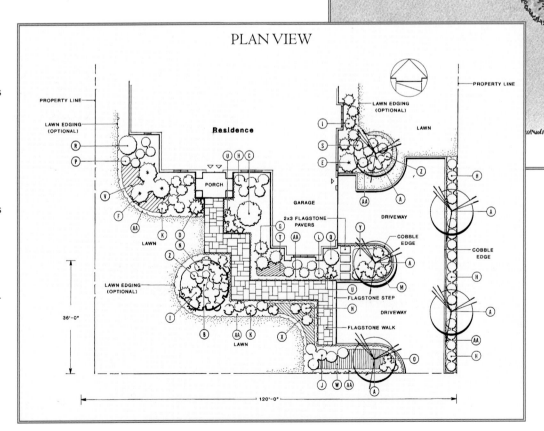

PLAN VIEW

All the trees in this landscape grow in beds and borders filled with groundcovers. The groundcovers smother weeds, absorb fallen leaves and keep trees healthy by protecting them from mower nicks.

BUBBLING FOUNTAIN

The delicately scented air allows you to envision a Provencal paradise. You can enjoy such sensory pleasures every day by installing this intricate design filled with fragrant plants. Be sure to provide plenty of seating around the patio so you'll have places to sit and enjoy the perfumed air. This plan is as adaptable as it is beautiful. The designer includes a patio and combination fountain/planter, but you could plant the border around any existing patio. You might decide to add only a central planter or fountain or both. You could locate the design right up against your house so that sliding glass or French doors open directly onto the patio—this allows you to enjoy the flowers' perfume from indoors as well. If you choose this option, site the planting so the lattice is directly opposite the wall of the house to capture and hold fragrance. The central planter and pots scattered about the patio are filled with fragrant annuals and tender perennials. During the cold winter months, try moving the pots to a sunny location inside the house, where they will continue to bloom and perfume the air.

DESIGN HPT220104

SHOWN IN SUMMER
Design by Jeffrey Diefenbach

REGIONALIZED PLANT LISTS

Because climate and growing conditions vary greatly throughout North America, it is impossible to list here specific plants for this landscape plan that would thrive in all regions of the country. However, you can order a Blueprint Package for this plan containing a list of plants selected by experts for your region.

The six-page Blueprint Package features a large-size version of this Plan View, plus a detailed Plant and Materials List. It also includes an illustrated list of hundreds of landscape plants suited to your region, to use if you wish to make substitutions, as well as planting instructions and plant adaptation maps to ensure professional-looking results.

See page 184 to order your regionalized Blueprint Package.

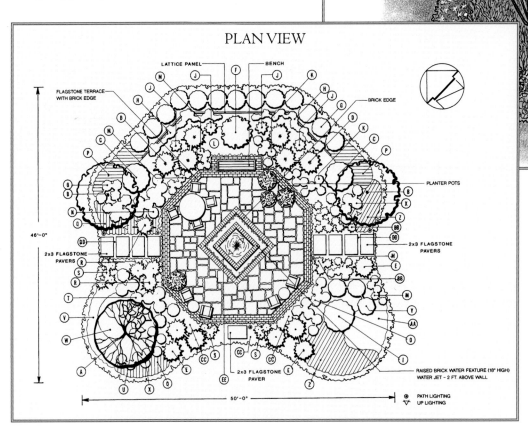

PLAN VIEW

Relaxing on this patio becomes a delightful sensory experience filled with sweet, flowery fragrances and the music of a bubbling fountain.

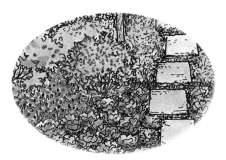

A mouth-watering, colorful and beautiful harvest is always close at hand when you plant this edible design near your front or back door.

ORNAMENTAL EDIBLES

Enjoy fresh herbs, vegetables and fruit from a large semicircular bed, brimming with beautiful edible plants. This plan is designed to be sited either against your house as an extension of your living space, or in any sunny place in your yard for dramatic impact. The garden's plants are chosen for their good looks as well as their edible qualities. Fruit trees provide shade and a fall harvest, while berry plants double as shrubbery. Smaller herbs, vegetables and fruits fill out the bed, offering food that can be eaten cooked or raw, used as seasoning, or made into tea. There's even one section devoted to a pretty salad garden. An informal flagstone terrace fills the center of the bed so you can easily putter in the garden or just sit and relax. Flagstone pavers divide the bed into smaller sections and lead into the garden's outer reaches to simplify harvesting and routine maintenance chores, such as weeding. The wooden arbors frame the terrace and create an interesting vertical effect while providing attractive supports for fruiting vines and climbing vegetables.

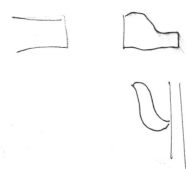

DESIGN HPT220105

SHOWN IN SUMMER
Design by Patrick J. Duffe

PLAN VIEW

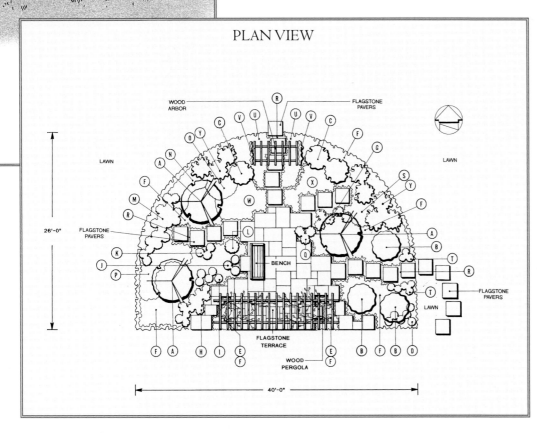

REGIONALIZED PLANT LISTS

Because climate and growing conditions vary greatly throughout North America, it is impossible to list here specific plants for this landscape plan that would thrive in all regions of the country. However, you can order a Blueprint Package for this plan containing a list of plants selected by experts for your region.

The six-page Blueprint Package features a large-size version of this Plan View, plus a detailed Plant and Materials List. It also includes an illustrated list of hundreds of landscape plants suited to your region, to use if you wish to make substitutions, as well as planting instructions and plant adaptation maps to ensure professional-looking results.

See page 184 to order your regionalized Blueprint Package.

RECOMMENDED READING

Following are groups of books that focus on Provence: travel memoirs, design books and travel guides. There are many more available in addition to those listed here; check your local bookstore or the World Wide Web to find more.

Life in Provence

If you're interested in learning more about the lifestyles and landscapes of Provence, try some of these travel memoirs and photographic essays.

by Peter Mayle

A Year in Provence
Toujours Provence
Encore Provence
French Lessons

Written by a British journalist who retreated to the French countryside, the first three books provide amusing anecdotes about good food, great wine and the quirky personalities that make up Provençal villages. The fourth, and most recent, is a gastronomic journey through all of France.

by Barrie Kerper (editor)

Provence: The Collected Traveler

Part of a series of anthologies that also includes books on Italy and Paris, this installment articles on French history along with tales of fine cuisine and wine tastings. Listings and reviews of places to go make this book a fine travel resource as well.

by Carol Drinkwater

The Olive Farm: A Memoir of Life, Love and Olive Oil in Southern France

A British actress provides another appealing portrait of life in Southern France after she and her husband purchase and renovate a villa near Cannes.

by Michael Jacobs

The Most Beautiful Villages of Provence

This book is part of a series of photographic essays, each focusing on a different picturesque region. Hugh Palmer's photographs offer a dramatic showcase of Provençal landscapes.

by Michel Biehn

Colors of Provence

Packed with full-color photography, this book celebrates the vivid colors that compose the Provençal landscape and find their way into its homes.

by Alexandra Bonfante-Warren

Timeless Places: Provence

With information on history, geography and tradition accompanied by beautiful photographs, this book is a visual tour of Provence.

Traveling to Provence

If you're planning to see the sights of Provence first-hand, let these books guide you. Many travel guides are updated every few years, so make sure that you select the most current one.

from Dorling-Kindersley (DK) Publishing

Eyewitness Travel Guides: Provence & the Côte d'Azur

This guide features over 800 full-color photographs and plenty of illustrations, along with listings of recommended hotels, restaurants and cafés.

from Michelin Travel Publications

The Green Guide: Provence

Maps, itineraries, and a rating system make this guide informative and indispensable.

from Knopf Guides

Provence & the Côte d'Azur

If you're interested in architecture, this may be the guide for you, with over 20 pages that concentrate on Provençal architecture.

from Lonely Planet

Provence & the Côte d'Azur

This down-to-earth guide focuses on information and begins with over 100 pages of information on general travel followed by facts specific to Provence.

from Cadogan Publishing, by Dana Facaros & Michael Pauls
Provence
This fun, informal guide offers a timeline of Provençal history.

from Fodor's
Escape to Provence, by Nancy Coons and Owen Franken
Provence & the Côte d'Azur
Escape to Provence is a new sort of travel guide, with lots of photography and brief descriptions of places you can go to celebrate Provençal traditions; Provence & the Côte d'Azur is the standard travel book, complete with maps and color photography.

from Frommer's
Provence & the Riviera
This guide provides information on places to stay for all price ranges, a glossary of French phrases and tips on regional dining.

Bringing Provence Home
To learn more about adding Provençal architecture and interior design to your home, try some of the following books.

by Betty Lou Phillips
Provençal Interiors: French Country Style in America
French by Design

by Barbara Buchholz and Lisa Skolnik
French Country (Architecture and Design Library)

by Cheryl MacLachlan
Bringing it Home: France

Draperies, wallpaper and upholstery are all the same playful pattern in this sitting room.

by Lisa Lovatt-Smith
Provence Interiors

by Daphne De Saint Sauveur
The French Touch: Decoration and Design in the Most Beautiful Homes of France

WEB RESOURCES

*Visit these Web sites for more information on Provence and the Côte d'Azur; each site also offers
plenty of links to take you to additional sites. Though some sites that focus on
Provence can only be viewed in French, a few are strictly in English and
many can be viewed in either English or French. Most sites that are
available in more than one language have helpful flag
icons to allow you to choose; click on the French
flag to display the page in French, and
the British or American flag to
see the page in
English.*

www.provenceweb.com: A comprehensive guide to touring Provence, with calendars of events, hotel and camping directories, a listing of recommended restaurants and much more. This site can be viewed in French or English.

www.provence-beyond.com: A very helpful site with plenty of information on Provence and its villages, with maps, guides to food and wines, lots of historical notes, and a message forum. This site is in English.

www.provencetourism: Another guide to touring Provence, with articles, a newsletter, an events calendar, and special information for business travelers. This site can be viewed in French, English and German.

www.visitprovence.com: A site that allows you to search by your area of interest, whether you're looking to plan a vacation or just learn more about Provence. This site can be viewed in English or French and also offers a selection of images so you can see the colors of Provence for yourself.

www.aboutprovence.com: Interviews with people who have traveled through Provence, listings of vacation and holiday rentals, and a Place-of-the-Month feature are some of this site's highlights. This site is in English.

www.guideweb.com/provence: Real estate listings, information about Provençal arts and crafts and regional products, and notes on history and geography are featured on this site, which is available in English and French.

www.saintremy-de-provence.com: Learn about the ancient architecture and modern shops and restaurants of Saint-Remy, where Vincent van Gogh lived for a time.

If you have a good command of the French language, you'll be able to view the following sites:

www.enprovence.com
www.laprovence.com
www.provence-online.com
www.aix-en-provence.com

MANUFACTURER RESOURCES

*Following is a listing of manufacturers that can help you add Provençal style to your home.
Call, write or visit their Web sites for catalogs and showroom or store locations.*

French Country Living
10135 Colvin Run Road
Great Falls, VA 22066
703-759-2245
www.frenchcountry.com

Pierre Deux
1-800-7-PIERRE
www.pierredeux.com

F. Schumacher & Co.
(Waverly and Village-brand fabrics)
1-800-552-9255
www.villagehome.com
www.waverly.com

Habersham Furniture Company
171 Collier Road
Toccoa, GA 30577
1-800-HABERSHAM
www.habershamdesigns.com

York Wallcoverings
750 Linden Ave.
P.O. Box 5166
York, PA 17405-5166
717-846-4456
www.yorkwall.com

Seabrook Wallcoverings
1325 Farmville Road
Memphis, TN 38122
1-800-238-9152
www.seabrookwallcoverings.com

Duralee Fabrics, Ltd.
www.duralee.com
1-800-ASK-DURA

Calico Corners
203 Gale Lane
Kennett Square, PA 19348-1764
1-800-213-6366
www.calicocorners.com

Souleiado
100 North Main Street
Chagrin Falls, Ohio 44022
440-247-8494
www.souleiadoshop.com

Brunschwig & Fils
914-684-5800
www.brunschwig.com

Simply Treasures Santons and French Collectibles
704-867-3728
www.simplytreasures.com

Le Paradou
1-800-256-7725
www.leparadou.com

Stroheim & Romann, Inc.
718-706-7000

This cheerful patio setting showcases the French tradition of harmoniously blending different prints and colors.

ACKNOWLEDGMENTS

Photographs and artwork were provided by the following manufacturers,
designers and photographers:

Robert Bailey: Front cover, 46-50, 192

Building Graphics: 56-59

Russ Collins: 3 (maps)

Digital Imagery ©2001 Photodisc, Inc.: Inside front cover, 5, 6-7, 8-9, 10-11, 17, 42-43

Duralee Fabrics, Ltd.: 26 (inset)

French Country Living: 25, 35

Habersham Furniture Company: 30 (inset)

International Homes of Cedar: 32

Le Paradou: 40 (top), 41 (bottom)

B. Massey Photographers: 60-63, back cover

Seabrook Wallcoverings: 20 (inset), 23, 38, 39, 177, back cover (inset)

Simply Treasures, Inc.: 40 (bottom), 41 (top and center)

Robert Starling: 51-55

Stephen Fuller, Inc: 20-21 (interior design by Mary McWilliams)

Stroheim & Romann, Inc.: 1, 22, 24, 26, 33, 34, 179

Stephen Trimble: 12, 14-15, 44, 45, 175-176

Village: 37

Waverly: 28, 29

York Wallcoverings: 27, 30, 31

LET US SHOW YOU OUR HOME BLUEPRINT PACKAGE.

BUILDING A HOME? PLANNING A HOME?
OUR BLUEPRINT PACKAGE HAS NEARLY EVERYTHING YOU NEED TO GET THE JOB DONE RIGHT,

whether you're working on your own or with help from an architect, designer, builder or subcontractors. Each Blueprint Package is the result of many hours of work by licensed architects or professional designers.

QUALITY

Hundreds of hours of painstaking effort have gone into the development of your blueprint set. Each home has been quality-checked by professionals to insure accuracy and buildability.

VALUE

Because we sell in volume, you can buy professional quality blueprints at a fraction of their development cost. With our plans, your dream home design costs substantially less than the fees charged by architects.

SERVICE

Once you've chosen your favorite home plan, you'll receive fast, efficient service whether you choose to mail or fax your order to us or call us toll free at 1-800-521-6797. For customer service, call toll free 1-888-690-1116.

SATISFACTION

Over 50 years of service to satisfied home plan buyers provide us unparalleled experience and knowledge in producing quality blueprints.

ORDER TOLL FREE
1-800-521-6797

After you've looked over our Blueprint Package and Important Extras, call toll free on our Blueprint Hotline: 1-800-521-6797, for current pricing and availability prior to mailing the order form on page 189. We're ready and eager to serve you. For customer service, call toll free 1-888-690-1116.

Each set of blueprints is an interrelated collection of detail sheets which includes components such as floor plans, interior and exterior elevations, dimensions, cross-sections, diagrams and notations. These sheets show exactly how your house is to be built.

SETS MAY INCLUDE:

FRONTAL SHEET
This artist's sketch of the exterior of the house gives you an idea of how the house will look when built and landscaped. Large floor plans show all levels of the house and provide an overview of your new home's livability, as well as a handy reference for deciding on furniture placement.

FOUNDATION PLANS
This sheet shows the foundation layout including support walls, excavated and unexcavated areas, if any, and foundation notes. If slab construction rather than basement, the plan shows footings and details for a monolithic slab. This page, or another in the set, may include a sample plot plan for locating your house on a building site.

DETAILED FLOOR PLANS
These plans show the layout of each floor of the house. Rooms and interior spaces are carefully dimensioned and keys are given for cross-section details provided later in the plans. The positions of electrical outlets and switches are shown.

HOUSE CROSS-SECTIONS
Large-scale views show sections or cut-aways of the foundation, interior walls, exterior walls, floors, stairways and roof details. Additional cross-sections may show important changes in floor, ceiling or roof heights or the relationship of one level to another. Extremely valuable for construction, these sections show exactly how the various parts of the house fit together.

INTERIOR ELEVATIONS
Many of our drawings show the design and placement of kitchen and bathroom cabinets, laundry areas, fireplaces, bookcases and other built-ins. Little "extras," such as mantelpiece and wainscoting drawings, plus molding sections, provide details that give your home that custom touch.

EXTERIOR ELEVATIONS
These drawings show the front, rear and sides of your house and give necessary notes on exterior materials and finishes. Particular attention is given to cornice detail, brick and stone accents or other finish items that make your home unique.

INTRODUCING EIGHT IMPORTANT

PLANNING AND CONSTRUCTION AIDS DEVELOPED BY

OUR PROFESSIONALS TO HELP YOU SUCCEED IN YOUR HOME-BUILDING PROJECT

MATERIALS LIST

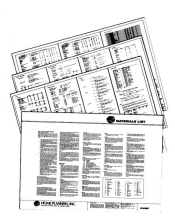

(Note: Because of the diversity of local building codes, our Materials List does not include mechanical materials.)

For many of the designs in our portfolio, we offer a customized materials take-off that is invaluable in planning and estimating the cost of your new home. This Materials List outlines the quantity, type and size of materials needed to build your house (with the exception of mechanical system items). Included are framing lumber, windows and doors, kitchen and bath cabinetry, rough and finish hardware, and much more. This handy list helps you or your builder cost out materials and serves as a reference sheet when you're compiling bids. A Materials List cannot be ordered before blueprints are ordered.

SPECIFICATION OUTLINE

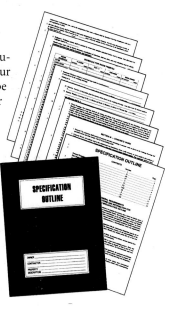

This valuable 16-page document is critical to building your house correctly. Designed to be filled in by you or your builder, this book lists 166 stages or items crucial to the building process. It provides a comprehensive review of the construction process and helps in choosing materials. When combined with the blueprints, a signed contract, and a schedule, it becomes a legal document and record for the building of your home.

QUOTE ONE®

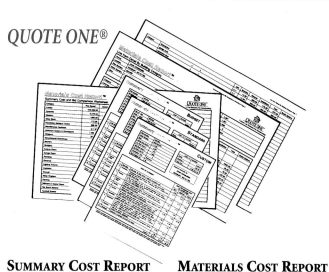

SUMMARY COST REPORT   MATERIALS COST REPORT

A product for estimating the cost of building select designs, the Quote One® system is available in two separate stages: The Summary Cost Report and the Materials Cost Report.

The **Summary Cost Report** is the first stage in the package and shows the total cost per square foot for your chosen home in your zip-code area and then breaks that cost down into various categories showing the costs for building materials, labor and installation. The report includes three grades: Budget, Standard and Custom. These reports allow you to evaluate your building budget and compare the costs of building a variety of homes in your area.

Make even more informed decisions about your home-building project with the second phase of our package, our **Materials Cost Report.** This tool is invaluable in planning and estimating the cost of your new home. The material and installation (labor and equipment) cost is shown for each of over 1,000 line items provided in the Materials List (Standard grade), which is included when you purchase this estimating tool. It allows you to determine building costs for your specific zip-code area and for your chosen home design. Space is allowed for additional estimates from contractors and subcontractors, such as for mechanical materials, which are not included in our packages. This invaluable tool includes a Materials List. A Materials Cost Report cannot be ordered before blueprints are ordered. Call for details. In addition, ask about our Home Planners Estimating Package.

If you are interested in a plan that is not indicated as Quote One®, please call and ask our sales reps. They will be happy to verify the status for you. To order these invaluable reports, use the order form on page 189 or call 1-800-521-6797 for availability.

CONSTRUCTION INFORMATION

IF YOU WANT TO KNOW MORE ABOUT TECHNIQUES— and deal more confidently with subcontractors — we offer these useful sheets. Each set is an excellent tool that will add to your understanding of these technical subjects. These helpful details provide general construction information and are not specific to any single plan.

PLUMBING

The Blueprint Package includes locations for all the plumbing fixtures, including sinks, lavatories, tubs, showers, toilets, laundry trays and water heaters. However, if you want to know more about the complete plumbing system, these Plumbing Details will prove very useful. Prepared to meet requirements of the National Plumbing Code, these fact-filled sheets give general information on pipe schedules, fittings, sump-pump details, water-softener hookups, septic system details and much more. Sheets also include a glossary of terms.

ELECTRICAL

The locations for every electrical switch, plug and outlet are shown in your Blueprint Package. However, these Electrical Details go further to take the mystery out of household electrical systems. Prepared to meet requirements of the National Electrical Code, these comprehensive drawings come packed with helpful information, including wire sizing, switch-installation schematics, cable-routing details, appliance wattage, doorbell hook-ups, typical service panel circuitry and much more. A glossary of terms is also included.

CONSTRUCTION

The Blueprint Package contains information an experienced builder needs to construct a particular house. However, it doesn't show all the ways that houses can be built, nor does it explain alternate construction methods. To help you understand how your house will be built—and offer additional techniques—this set of Construction Details depicts the materials and methods used to build foundations, fireplaces, walls, floors and roofs. Where appropriate, the drawings show acceptable alternatives.

MECHANICAL

These Mechanical Details contain fundamental principles and useful data that will help you make informed decisions and communicate with subcontractors about heating and cooling systems. Drawings contain instructions and samples that allow you to make simple load calculations, and preliminary sizing and costing analysis. Covered are the most commonly used systems from heat pumps to solar fuel systems. The package is filled with illustrations and diagrams to help you visualize components and how they relate to one another.

PLAN-A-HOME®

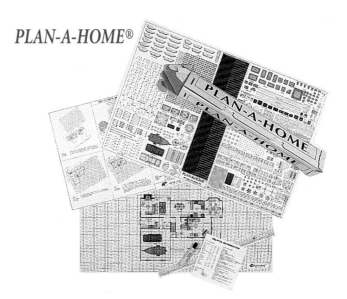

PLAN-A-HOME® is an easy-to-use tool that helps you design a new home, arrange furniture in a new or existing home, or plan a remodeling project. Each package contains:

✓ **More than 700 reusable peel-off planning symbols** on a self-stick vinyl sheet, including walls, windows, doors, all types of furniture, kitchen components, bath fixtures and many more.

✓ **A reusable, transparent, ¼" scale planning grid** that matches the scale of actual working drawings (¼" equals one foot). This grid provides the basis for house layouts of up to 140' x 92'.

✓ **Tracing paper** and a protective sheet for copying or transferring your completed plan.

✓ **A felt-tip pen**, with water-soluble ink that wipes away quickly.

PLAN-A-HOME® lets you lay out areas as large as a 7,500 square foot, six-bedroom, seven-bath house.

To Order, Call Toll Free
1-800-521-6797

After you've looked over our Blueprint Package and Important Extras on these pages, call toll free on our Blueprint Hotline: 1-800-521-6797 for current pricing and availability prior to mailing the order form on page 189. We're ready and eager to serve you. For customer service, call toll free 1-888-690-1116.

THE DECK BLUEPRINT PACKAGE

Many of the homes in this book can be enhanced with a professionally designed Home Planners Deck Plan. Those home plans highlighted with a **D** have a matching Deck Plan, sold separately, which includes a Deck Plan Frontal Sheet, Deck Framing and Floor Plans, Deck Elevations and a Deck Materials List. A Standard Deck Details Package, also available, provides all the how-to information necessary for building *any* deck. Our Complete Deck Building Package contains one set of Custom Deck Plans of your choice, plus one set of Standard Deck Building Details, all for one low price. Our plans and details are carefully prepared in an easy-to-understand format that will guide you through every stage of your deck-building project. This page shows a sample of Deck layouts to match your favorite house. See page 185 for prices and ordering information.

THE LANDSCAPE BLUEPRINT PACKAGE

For the homes marked with an **L** in this book, Home Planners has created a front-yard Landscape Plan that matches or is complementary in design to the house plan. These comprehensive blueprint packages include a Frontal Sheet, Plan View, Regionalized Plant & Materials List, a sheet on Planting and Maintaining Your Landscape, Zone Maps and Plant Size and Description Guide. These plans will help you achieve professional results, adding value and enjoyment to your property for years to come. Each set of blueprints is a full 18" x 24" in size with clear, complete instructions and easy-to-read type. A sample Landscape Plan is shown below.

CONTEMPORARY LEISURE DECK
Deck ODA021

CAPE COD COTTAGE
Landscape OLA003

Regional Order Map

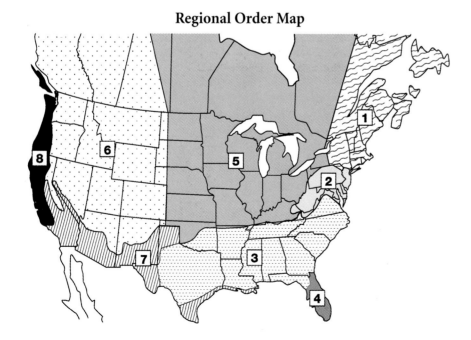

Most Landscape Plans are available with a Plant & Materials List adapted by horticultural experts to 8 different regions of the country. Please specify the Geographic Region when ordering your plan. See pages 185–187 for prices, ordering information and regional availability.

Region	1	Northeast
Region	2	Mid-Atlantic
Region	3	Deep South
Region	4	Florida & Gulf Coast
Region	5	Midwest
Region	6	Rocky Mountains
Region	7	Southern California & Desert Southwest
Region	8	Northern California & Pacific Northwest

HOUSE BLUEPRINT PRICE SCHEDULE
Prices guaranteed through December 31, 2002

TIERS	1-SET STUDY PACKAGE	4-SET BUILDING PACKAGE	8-SET BUILDING PACKAGE	1-SET REPRODUCIBLE
P1	$20	$50	$90	$140
P2	$40	$70	$110	$160
P3	$70	$100	$140	$190
P4	$100	$130	$170	$220
P5	$140	$170	$210	$270
P6	$180	$210	$250	$310
A1	$440	$480	$520	$660
A2	$480	$520	$560	$720
A3	$520	$560	$600	$780
A4	$565	$605	$645	$850
C1	$610	$655	$700	$915
C2	$655	$700	$745	$980
C3	$700	$745	$790	$1050
C4	$750	$795	$840	$1125
L1	$825	$875	$925	$1240
L2	$900	$950	$1000	$1340
L3	$1000	$1095	$1100	$1500
L4	$1100	$1150	$1200	$1650

OPTIONS FOR PLANS IN TIERS A1–L4

Additional Identical Blueprints
in same order for "A1–L4" price plans ....**$50 per set**
Reverse Blueprints (mirror image)
with 4- or 8-set order for "A1–L4" plans...............................**$50 fee per order**
Specification Outlines...**$10 each**
Materials Lists for "A1–C3" plans ....**$60 each**
Materials Lists for "C4–L4" plans...**$70 each**

OPTIONS FOR PLANS IN TIERS P1–P6

Additional Identical Blueprints
in same order for "P1–P6" price plans...**$10 per set**
Reverse Blueprints (mirror image) for "P1–P6" price plans ....**$10 per set**
1 Set of Deck Construction Details ....**$14.95 each**
Deck Construction Package ....**add $10 to Building Package price**
(includes 1 set of "P1–P6" plans, plus
1 set Standard Deck Construction Details)
1 Set of Gazebo Construction Details ....**$14.95 each**
Gazebo Construction Package ....**add $10 to Building Package price**
(includes 1 set of "P1–P6" plans, plus 1 set
Standard Gazebo Construction Details)

IMPORTANT NOTES
• The 1-set study package is marked "not for construction."
• Prices for 4- or 8-set Building Packages honored only at time of original order.
• Some foundations carry a $225 surcharge.
• Right-reading reverse blueprints, if available, will incur a $165 surcharge.
• Additional identical blueprints may be purchased within 60 days of original order.

TO USE THE INDEX, refer to the design number listed in numerical order (a helpful page reference is also given). Note the price tier and refer to the House Blueprint Price Schedule above for the cost of one, four or eight sets of blueprints or the cost of a reproducible drawing. Additional prices are shown for identical and reverse blueprint sets, as well as a very useful Materials List for some of the plans. Also note in the Plan Index, those plans that have Deck Plans or Landscape Plans. Refer to the schedules above for prices of these plans. The letter "Y" identifies plans that are part of our Quote One® estimating service and those that offer Materials Lists. See page 182 for more information.

TO ORDER, Call toll free 1-800-521-6797 or 520-297-8200 for current pricing and availability prior to mailing the order form on page 189. FAX: 1-800-224-6699 or 520-544-3086.

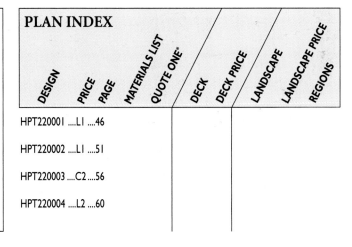

PLAN INDEX

DESIGN	PRICE	PAGE	MATERIALS LIST	QUOTE ONE®	DECK	DECK PRICE	LANDSCAPE	LANDSCAPE PRICE	REGIONS
HPT220001	L1	46							
HPT220002	L1	51							
HPT220003	C2	56							
HPT220004	L2	60							

BEFORE FILLING OUT THE ORDER FORM, PLEASE CALL US ON OUR TOLL-FREE BLUEPRINT HOTLINE, YOU MAY WANT TO LEARN MORE ABOUT OUR SERVICES AND PRODUCTS. HERE'S SOME INFORMATION YOU WILL FIND HELPFUL.

OUR EXCHANGE POLICY

With the exception of reproducible plan orders, we will exchange your entire first order for an equal or greater number of blueprints within our plan collection within 90 days of the original order. The entire content of your original order must be returned before an exchange will be processed. Please call our customer service department for your return authorization number and shipping instructions. If the returned blueprints look used, redlined or copied, we will not honor your exchange. Fees for exchanging your blueprints are as follows: 20% of the amount of the original order...plus the difference in cost if exchanging for a design in a higher price bracket or less the difference in cost if exchanging for a design in a lower price bracket. **(Reproducible blueprints are not exchangeable or refundable.)** Please call for current postage and handling prices. Shipping and handling charges are not refundable.

ABOUT REVERSE BLUEPRINTS

Although lettering and dimensions will appear backward, reverses will be a useful aid if you decide to flop the plan. See Price Schedule and Plans Index for pricing.

REVISING, MODIFYING AND CUSTOMIZING PLANS

Like many homeowners who buy these plans, you and your builder, architect or engineer may want to make changes to them. We recommend purchase of a reproducible plan for any changes made by your builder, licensed architect or engineer. As set forth below, we cannot assume any responsibility for blueprints which have been changed, whether by you, your builder or by professionals selected by you or referred to you by us, because such individuals are outside our supervision and control.

ARCHITECTURAL AND ENGINEERING SEALS

Some cities and states are now requiring that a licensed architect or engineer review and "seal" a blueprint, or officially approve it, prior to construction due to concerns over energy costs, safety and other factors. Prior to application for a building permit or the start of actual construction, we strongly advise that you consult your local building official who can tell you if such a review is required.

ABOUT THE DESIGNS

The architects and designers whose work appears in this publication are among America's leading residential designers. Each plan was designed to meet the requirements of a nationally recognized model building code in effect at the time and place the plan was drawn. Because national building codes change from time to time, plans may not comply with any such code at the time they are sold to a customer. In addition, building officials may not accept these plans as final construction documents of record as the plans may need to be modified and additional drawings and details added to suit local conditions and requirements. We strongly advise that purchasers consult a licensed architect or engineer, and their local building official, before starting any construction related to these plans.

LOCAL BUILDING CODES AND ZONING REQUIREMENTS

At the time of creation, our plans are drawn to specifications published by the Building Officials and Code Administrators (BOCA) International, Inc.; the Southern Building Code Congress (SBCCI) International, Inc.; the International Conference of Building Officials (ICBO); or the Council of American Building Officials (CABO). Our plans are designed to meet or exceed national building standards. Because of the great differences in geography and climate throughout the United States and Canada, each state, county and municipality has its own building codes, zone requirements, ordinances and building regulations. Your plan may need to be modified to comply with local requirements regarding snow loads, energy codes, soil and seismic conditions and a wide range of other matters. In addition, you may need to obtain permits or inspections from local governments before and in the course of construction. Prior to using blueprints ordered from us, we strongly advise that you consult a licensed architect or engineer—and speak with your local building official—before applying for any permit or beginning construction. We authorize the use of our blueprints on the express condition that you strictly comply with all local building codes, zoning requirements and other applicable laws, regulations, ordinances and requirements. Notice: Plans for homes to be built in Nevada must be re-drawn by a Nevada-registered professional. Consult your building official for more information on this subject.

DISCLAIMER

The designers we work with have put substantial care and effort into the creation of their blueprints. However, because they cannot provide on-site consultation, supervision and control over actual construction, and because of the great variance in local building requirements, building practices and soil, seismic, weather and other conditions, WE CANNOT MAKE ANY WARRANTY, EXPRESS OR IMPLIED, WITH RESPECT TO THE CONTENT OR USE OF THE BLUEPRINTS, INCLUDING BUT NOT LIMITED TO ANY WARRANTY OF MERCHANTABILITY OR OF FITNESS FOR A PARTICULAR PURPOSE. **ITEMS, PRICES, TERMS AND CONDITIONS ARE SUBJECT TO CHANGE WITHOUT NOTICE. REPRODUCIBLE PLAN ORDERS MAY REQUIRE A CUSTOMER'S SIGNED RELEASE BEFORE SHIPPING.**

TERMS AND CONDITIONS

These designs are protected under the terms of United States Copyright Law and may not be copied or reproduced in any way, by any means, unless you have purchased Reproducibles which clearly indicate your right to copy or reproduce. We authorize the use of your chosen design as an aid in the construction of one single family home only. You may not use this design to build a second or multiple dwellings without purchasing another blueprint or blueprints or paying additional design fees.

HOW MANY BLUEPRINTS DO YOU NEED?

Although a standard building package may satisfy many states, cities and counties, some plans may require certain changes. For your convenience, we have developed a Reproducible plan which allows a local professional to modify and make up to 10 copies of your revised plan. As our plans are all copyright protected, with your purchase of the Reproducible, we will supply you with a Copyright release letter. The number of copies you may need, 1 for owner; 3 for builder; 2 for local building department and 1-3 sets for your mortgage lender.

ORDER TOLL FREE!
FOR INFORMATION ABOUT ANY OF OUR SERVICES OR TO ORDER CALL

1-800-521-6797
OR **520-297-8200**
Browse our website:
www.eplans.com

BLUEPRINTS ARE NOT REFUNDABLE EXCHANGES ONLY

FOR CUSTOMER SERVICE,
CALL TOLL FREE **1-888-690-1116**.

HOME PLANNERS, LLC wholly owned by Hanley-Wood, LLC
3275 WEST INA ROAD, SUITE 110 • TUCSON, ARIZONA • 85741

THE BASIC BLUEPRINT PACKAGE
Rush me the following (please refer to the Plans Index and Price Schedule in this section):
___Set(s) of blueprints, plan number(s) _____ indicate foundation type _____ $_____
___Set(s) of reproducibles, plan number(s) _____ indicate foundation type _____ $_____
___Additional identical blueprints (standard or reverse) in same order @ $50 per set. $_____
___Reverse blueprints @ $50 fee per order. Right-reading reverse @ $165 surcharge $_____

IMPORTANT EXTRAS
Rush me the following:
___Materials List: $60 (Must be purchased with Blueprint set.) Add $10 for Schedule C4–L4 plans. $_____
___**Quote One**® Summary Cost Report @ $29.95 for one, $14.95 for each additional,
　　for plans _____ $_____
　　Building location: City _____ Zip Code _____
___**Quote One**® Materials Cost Report @ $120 Schedules P1–C3; $130 Schedules C4–L4,
　　for plan_____(Must be purchased with Blueprints set.) $_____
　　Building location: City _____ Zip Code _____
___Specification Outlines @ $10 each. $_____
___Detail Sets @ $14.95 each; any two $22.95; any three $29.95; all four for $39.95 (save $19.85). $_____
　　❏ Plumbing ❏ Electrical ❏ Construction ❏ Mechanical
___Plan-A-Home® @ $29.95 each. $_____

DECK BLUEPRINTS
(Please refer to the Plans Index and Price Schedule in this section)
___Set(s) of Deck Plan _____. $_____
___Additional identical blueprints in same order @ $10 per set. $_____
___Reverse blueprints @ $10 fee per order. $_____
___Set of Standard Deck Details @ $14.95 per set. $_____
___Set of Complete Deck Construction Package (Best Buy!) Add $10 to Building Package
　　Includes Custom Deck Plan _____ Plus Standard Deck Details

LANDSCAPE BLUEPRINTS
(Please refer to the Plans Index and Price Schedule in this section)
___Set(s) of Landscape Plan _____. $_____
___Additional identical blueprints in same order @ $10 per set. $_____
___Reverse blueprints @ $10 fee per order. $_____
Please indicate the appropriate region of the country for Plant & Material List.
(See map on page 184): Region _____

POSTAGE AND HANDLING	1–3 sets	4+ sets
Signature is required for all deliveries. **DELIVERY** No CODs (Requires street address—No P.O. Boxes)		
•Regular Service (Allow 7–10 business days delivery)	❏ $20.00	❏ $25.00
•Priority (Allow 4–5 business days delivery)	❏ $25.00	❏ $35.00
•Express (Allow 3 business days delivery)	❏ $35.00	❏ $45.00
OVERSEAS DELIVERY	fax, phone or mail for quote	

Note: All delivery times are from date Blueprint Package is shipped.

POSTAGE (From box above) $_____
SUBTOTAL $_____
SALES TAX (AZ & MI residents, please add appropriate state and local sales tax.) $_____
TOTAL (Subtotal and tax) $_____

YOUR ADDRESS (please print legibly)

Name _____

Street_____

City _____State_____Zip _____

Daytime telephone number (required) (_____) _____

FOR CREDIT CARD ORDERS ONLY

Credit card number _____ Exp. Date: (M/Y) _____
Check one ❏ Visa ❏ MasterCard ❏ Discover Card ❏ American Express

Order Form Key
HPT22

Signature (required) _____

Please check appropriate box: ❏ Licensed Builder-Contractor ❏ Homeowner

ORDER TOLL FREE!
1-800-521-6797 or 520-297-8200
BY FAX: Copy the order form above and send it on our FAXLINE: 1-800-224-6699 OR 1-520-544-3086

HOME PLANNERS WANTS YOUR BUILDING EXPERIENCE TO BE AS PLEASANT AND TROUBLE-FREE AS POSSIBLE.

That's why we've expanded our library of Do-It-Yourself titles to help you along. In addition to our beautiful plans books, we've added books to guide you through specific projects as well as the construction process. In fact, these are titles that will be as useful after your dream home is built as they are right now.

BIGGEST & BEST	ONE-STORY	MORE ONE-STORY	TWO-STORY	VACATION	HILLSIDE	FARMHOUSE	COUNTRY HOUSES

| **1** 1001 of our best-selling plans in one volume. 1,074 to 7,275 square feet. 704 pgs $12.95 1K1 | **2** 450 designs for all lifestyles. 800 to 4,900 square feet. 384 pgs $9.95 OS | **3** 475 superb one-level plans from 800 to 5,000 square feet. 448 pgs $9.95 MOS | **4** 443 designs for one-and-a-half and two stories. 1,500 to 6,000 square feet. 448 pgs $9.95 TS | **5** 465 designs for recreation, retirement and leisure. 448 pgs $9.95 VSH | **6** 208 designs for split-levels, bi-levels, multi-levels and walkouts. 224 pgs $9.95 HH | **7** 200 country designs from classic to contemporary by 7 winning designers. 224 pgs $8.95 FH | **8** 208 unique home plans that combine traditional style and modern livability. 224 pgs $9.95 CN |

BUDGET-SMART	BARRIER FREE	ENCYCLOPEDIA	ENCYCLOPEDIA II	AFFORDABLE	VICTORIAN	ESTATE	LUXURY

| **9** 200 efficient plans from 7 top designers, that you can really afford to build! 224 pgs $8.95 BS | **10** Over 1,700 products and 51 plans for accessible living. 128 pgs $15.95 UH | **11** 500 exceptional plans for all styles and budgets—the best book of its kind! 528 pgs $9.95 ENC | **12** 500 completely new plans. Spacious and stylish designs for every budget and taste. 352 pgs $9.95 E2 | **13** Completely revised and updated, featuring 300 designs for modest budgets. 256 pgs $9.95 AF | **14** NEW! 210 striking Victorian and Farmhouse designs from today's top designers. 224 pgs $15.95 VDH2 | **15** Twen... | |

EUROPEAN STYLES	COUNTRY CLASSICS	WILLIAM POOLE	TRADITIONAL	COTTAGES	CLASSIC	CO...	

| **17** 200 homes with a unique flair of the Old World. 224 pgs $15.95 EURO | **18** Donald Gardner's 101 best Country and Traditional home plans. 192 pgs $17.95 DAG | **19** 70 romantic house plans that capture the classic tradition of home design. 160 pgs $17.95 WEP | **20** 85 timeless designs from the Design Traditions Library. 160 pgs $17.95 TRA | **21** 25 fresh new designs that are as warm as a tropical breeze. A blend of the best aspects of many coastal styles. 64 pgs $19.95 CTG | **22** Timeless, elegant designs that always feel like home. Gorgeous plans that are flexible and up-to-date as their occupants. 240 pgs $9.95 CS | **23** ...lection of contemporary designs available anywhere. 240 pgs. $9.95 CM | ...and... that are small in size, but big on livability. 224 pgs $8.95 EL |

SOUTHERN	SOUTHWESTERN	WESTERN	NEIGHBORHOOD	CRAFTSMAN	COLONIAL HOUSES	DUPLEX & TOWNHOMES	WATERFRONT

| **25** 207 homes rich in Southern styling and comfort. 240 pgs $8.95 SH | **26** 138 designs that capture the spirit of the Southwest. 144 pgs $10.95 SW | **27** 215 designs that capture the spirit and diversity of the Western lifestyle. 208 pgs $9.95 WH | **28** 170 designs with the feel of main street America. 192 pgs $12.95 TND | **29** 170 Home plans in the Craftsman and Bungalow style. 192 pgs $12.95 CC | **30** 181 Classic early American designs. 208 pgs $9.95 COL | **31** Over 50 designs for multi-family living. 64 pgs $9.95 DTP | **32** 200 designs perfect for your waterside wonderland. 208 pgs $10.95 WF |